HAZARDOUS
PURSUIT

2012

To Zane
My RCMP
Grandson to be."

Enjoy and
+ Support

Love

Always

GMA

HAZARDOUS PURSUIT

Bruce Strachan

CAITLIN PRESS
1995

Hazardous Pursuit
Copyright © 1995 Bruce Strachan

Caitlin Press Inc.
P.O. Box 2387, Stn. B
Prince George, B.C. V2N 2S6

Caitlin Press gratefully acknowledges the financial support of the Canada Council and the British Columbia Cultural Services Branch, Ministry of Tourism, Small Business and Culture.

Canadian Cataloguing in Publication Data

Strachan, Bruce, 1941-
  Hazardous Pursuit

  Includes index.
  ISBN 0-920576-55-9

  1. Police shootings--British Columbia. 2. Public relations--Police--British Columbia. 3. Royal Canadian Mounted Police.
I. Title.
HV8159.B75S77 1995   363.2'32   C95-910506-9

 PRINTED IN CANADA

Contents

Foreword

THIS STORY IS ABSOLUTELY TRUE. Every word of dialogue you'll read is taken from RCMP transcripts, the evidence given at the coroner's inquest and interviews the author had with those involved.

The shootings are real. Two young men died and seasoned police officers wept when they talked about the tragedy of death.

By way of acknowledgment, I first want to thank Kathy James for her help. She talked to me about Russell Michell in a way that only a wife could. I wish Kathy and her children all the best for their future.

When I began my research, I was told by friends in the RCMP that police officers don't take kindly to answering questions, especially from freelance writers who are former politicians. Having said that, I must acknowledge all the help, official and otherwise, I had from the RCMP, particularly from Sergeant Al Olsen, who went through a period of considerable personal turmoil.

It took Al Olsen some time to confide in me and, given the circumstances, I can't say I blame him. Prior to the coroner's inquest, he was under considerable pressure, feeling with some justification that his judgment as a police officer was being compromised by political expediencies.

Constables Stan Walstrom of the RCMP and Keith McKay of the Lillooet Tribal Police were the first two officers in the pursuit and their assistance was invaluable. My thanks to them for their candor.

Superintendent Len Olfert of the RCMP Kamloops Subdivision and Sergeant Peter Montague, E Division, Vancouver, were also particularly helpful.

In Prince George I was provided with much good advice from RCMP media relations officer Constable Gordon Molendyke. Whenever I asked, Gordon provided me with copies and explanations of RCMP policy. It was through Gordon that I had the opportunity to drive a police car, giving me a better understanding of the heavy duty handling package. Finally, Gordon Molendyke was good enough, and I guess trusting enough, to give me a "hands on" lesson on the electric latch mechanism that releases a police car shotgun.

Thanks also to Telecoms Directors Stevie Sharon in Kamloops and Terry Edwards in Prince George. The RCMP communications system is a critical investigative tool and it was essential for me to understand how it operated.

Prince George pathologist, Dr. Jennifer Rice was especially kind, listening patiently to my questions and providing me with quick and easily understood anatomy lessons whenever I called on her for advice.

In Lillooet I received a great deal of excellent background information. First and foremost from *Bridge River Lillooet News* editor and reporter Christ'l Roshard, who was tremendously helpful. Christ'l is a powerful writer and helped me focus on the human tragedy that is so much a part of life for native people. I also have to thank Corporal Fred Pearson of the RCMP Lillooet Detachment for his assistance.

Many of my references to the history of the Lillooet Nation come from an excellent work by Joanne Drake-Terry, titled *The Same As Yesterday*. Joanne is the wife of Saul Terry, chief of the Bridge River Indian Band and president of the Union of BC Indian Chiefs.

Following the inquest, Regional Coroner Bob Graham gave me unlimited access to all the evidence provided to the coroner's court. This material was essential. Not only did it provide the cold clinical details of death, it also described how the loss of a loved one has an impact on so many.

Hazardous Pursuit took over a year to write, partly because of continued delays in setting the date for the coroner's inquest, but due as well to the difficulty of assembling a complete picture from the mountains of information provided to me. I want, as well, to thank Caitlin Press for their patience and editors David Speck and Susan Rothstein for their patience and excellent advice.

Hazardous Pursuit is about more than just a sixty seven kilometre ride along a treacherous ice-covered logging road carved out of the West Pavilion hills. Sadly, this book also tells of an event that characterizes the hopelessness of life for so many of Canada's aboriginal population.

There are no heroes on these pages. Rather, the events that swept up Randy Monk, Rusty Michell, Al Olsen, Stan Walstrom and Keith McKay are disturbing reflections of our society's failure to deal with the angry frustration felt by so many young native Indians.

We have condemned native people to life on reserves, stripped away the connections to their heritage and given them no hope for the future. Then we send armed police officers to protect us when the anguish and outrage of over a century of injustice turns violently against us.

It is my hope that this book will help us better understand that anger and challenge us to pursue solutions.

This book is dedicated to all those who were so supportive. But particularly to all the members of my family who stood by me over the last year. Their support was essential to the project.

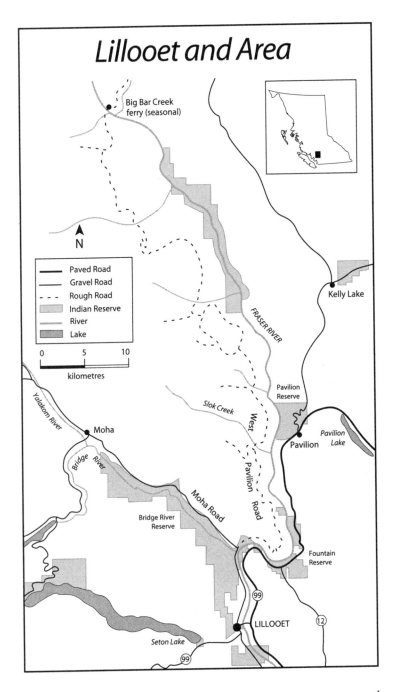

Lil1ooet and Area

Big Bar Creek
ferry (seasonal)

N

Kelly Lake

Paved Road
Gravel Road
Rough Road
Indian Reserve
River
Lake

FRASER RIVER

0   5   10
kilometres

Pavilion
Reserve

Slok Creek

Moha

Pavilion

Pavilion
Lake

Yalakom River

West

Bridge River

Pavilion Road

Moha Road

Bridge River
Reserve

Fountain
Reserve

99

99

Seton Lake

LILLOOET

12

The rugged West Pavilion Hills above the Fraser River.

1

LILLOOET, BRITISH COLUMBIA, is set on benchlands that rise from the confluence of the Fraser and Bridge rivers. Located two hours north of the famed Whistler ski resort and an hour away from Highway 97 to the north and the Trans-Canada highway to the south, Lillooet enjoys its valley seclusion. Long-time residents say their community is one of the best-kept secrets in British Columbia.

The setting is pleasant, yet rugged. From the river bottoms, Fountain Ridge rises to the east and Mission Ridge and Mount McLean to the west. Ponderosa pine provide a sparse cover in places and sagebrush grows where the dusty soil is too thin for trees.

Although Lillooet is removed from the more well-traveled highways, it's situated on the mainline of the British Columbia Railway. During the summer months, self-propelled rail cars bring visitors from North Vancouver up scenic Howe Sound through the rugged Coast Mountain Range to Lillooet. The railway crews stage mock train robberies, and everyone has a great time reliving and acting out the past.

Those tourists who drive to the Lillooet area come for the warm summers, the outdoor recreation and the fishing. The waters are abundant with many varieties of trout and in the deep pools of the Fraser River, sturgeon weighing up to 1,000 pounds have been landed.

During the summer and fall stock-car racing adds to the noise and excitement. Racing teams come up from Vancouver and the adjoining BC Interior communities to pound around the quarter-mile track and thrill local racing fans. The throaty, rapping sound of modified V-8s and V-6s with high-lift camshafts and lightly restricted exhaust systems echoes through the valley for miles.

For those months, Lillooet is warm and dry, an inviting retreat. The hills surrounding Lillooet climb steeply from the rivers. But on the east side of the Fraser, and farther north on both sides, there are flat benchlands where enterprising farmers grow ginseng, the most profitable legal agricultural crop cultivated in North America. During the hot summer months, the pampered ginseng roots grow under the cover of black polypropylene tarpaulins. Literally acres upon acres of flat black synthetic canopy cover the crop. In its natural habitat, ginseng grows in the cover of hardwood trees and so like leaves the tarps have been designed to shade the plants from the beating Fraser Canyon summer sunshine.

After Labour Day, the tourist traffic begins to slow. By mid-October, the ginseng tarpaulins are rolled back, letting the full heat of the fall sun warm the earth and the ginseng crop.

When the stock-car races end, Lillooet is left to listen to diesel logging trucks with their rapping engine brakes, and to the never-ending rumble of the heavy BC Rail diesel-electric freight trains that wind north and south on tracks clinging precariously to the rocky hills.

Winter comes, snow falls, there's less to do, the heat of the sun is gone, and soon so is another year. The rocky, pine-covered hills surrounding Lillooet no longer bake in the summer sun, but sit cold, brooding and quiet.

The Lillooet Nation has a rich history. Before the Europeans came to the river valleys, the aboriginal peoples enjoyed unlimited access to waters rich with salmon and land abundant in game.

The hot windy summers allowed the natives to air-dry the plentiful salmon catch and either store it for the winter or to use for trade with other tribes. It was common for the Shuswap and Nlaka'pamux peoples to come to the Lillooet territory and trade buffalo skins, roots and berries for the wind-dried salmon. Mule deer were plentiful and trapping was an all-year round activity, since the winter weather was moderate, the Lillooet people wintered comfortably in sod-covered pithouses.

The first white man seen by the Lillooet people was Simon Fraser. In 1808, he came south through Lillooet on the river that was to bear his name. Although Simon Fraser was the first white man to visit the river valleys, he was by no means the last.

By the 1850s, thousands of fortune seekers on their way north to the Barkerville gold fields had travelled up the Fraser River through Lillooet. With the white man came smallpox, by 1886 two thirds of the Lillooet nation had died from the disease.

Well before the turn of the century, the Lillooet flat lands were being taken up by white settlers while the Ca-

Top: *The exterior entrance of a reconstructed pithouse.*
Above: *Interior of pithouse.*

nadian government relegated the Indians to reserves. These reserves were not the native's own land, with title and some sense of territorial ownership, but rather ghetto-like plots described in the cold bureaucratic language of turn-of-the-century Victorian Canada as, "Federal lands reserved for the Indians."

Having taken the natives' land, the white governments of the day next took steps to ensure that natives were assimilated into the white society. In the late 1880s, the federal Indian affair department began forcibly removing native children from their homes and sending them to church-run residential schools. Here they were to learn English, the Catechism and most importantly the "work ethic" of the white settlers. It was a Canadian rendition of ethnic cleansing.

The policy was a disaster. The residential schools didn't help the natives to assimilate; they only stressed the significant differences between the native and white societies while stripping away what little cultural pride the Indians had left.

2

THE BRIDGE RIVER INDIAN RESERVE, north of Lillooet BC Christmas Eve. December 24, 1993. 19:42 Hours. The call was to the Royal Canadian Mounted Police Telecommunications Centre in Kamloops, British Columbia. Referred to as Telecoms, the centre handles all incoming calls in the RCMP Kamloops Subdivision. The Telecoms operator taking the call was Debbie Mills, a civilian employee of the RCMP. The female caller sounded frightened, nervous, or both. As it turned out, she was terrified for herself and her five children. It was a desperate call.

"Can I get some help up here at the Bridge River, Riv . . . Bridge River Reserve?'

Mills responded, "Bridge River Reserve? What's going on up there?

"He's trashing the house."

"OK. What's your last name?"

"James, Kathy James. Hurry, my kids are over there!"

Debbie Mills needed more information to do a record check. "What's his name?"

"Russell Michell."

"And how old is he?"

"Thirty-one."

And as Debbie Mills was soon to find out when she ran a record check, Russell Thomas (Rusty) Michell was a violent young man who had crowded a lot hard living into his life. Born May 30, 1962, to Raphael and Flora Michell on the Bridge River Reserve, Rusty was the ninth of ten children in the Michell family.

He had a rough start right from the beginning. His home life, like that of so many native children, was typically distressing. There was too much drinking, too many abusive situations, rampant chronic unemployment and the poorest of living conditions.

To add to his problems, Rusty was a small child and didn't reach normal growth until he was well into his midteens. When Rusty was twelve, his mother Flora suffered a paralyzing stroke. Russell's father, Raphael, unable and quite unprepared to look after the young lad, had him sent away to the Indian residential school in Kamloops. There, Rusty was constantly and cruelly teased about his height. In a classic Napoleon-complex response, Rusty fought back and he fought back hard. He picked fights; some he won, a lot he lost, but he never backed down.

Following Flora's stroke and for the summer months when he wasn't at residential school, Russell began living with foster parents Carole and Fred John on the Fountain Band Reserve. Fred and Carole were kind, caring people, but they couldn't control Rusty's hair-trigger anger.

On one of Rusty's stays with the John family, and for no apparent reason, he picked up a two-by-four piece of lumber and brutally clubbed an old man who lived next door to the John's home. During his teenage years Rusty spent a great deal of time in juvenile detention centres for break and enter, theft and assault. At times the rage inside him threatened to overwhelm him. When this happened, he'd often leave his foster home and go alone into the mountains for two to three days. Rusty Michell would often talk to Fred John about getting away and being alone. The understanding foster parent knew that Rusty's retreats to the mountains were a way of dealing with his anger and erasing the abusive memories of his youth. A spiritual and healing journey away from the ghetto life of Indian reserves, residential schools and the seemingly hopeless future facing young natives like Rusty. Fred John also knew these retreats were Rusty's way of dealing with his anger and erasing the bitter memories of his youth.

A week after his eighteenth birthday, Rusty Michell found himself in jail once more, this time serving nine months concurrent on convictions for break and enter theft, break and enter with intent and possession of a weapon.

And as Kathy James made her Christmas Eve call to the RCMP, Rusty Michell already had an extensive criminal record, including numerous charges for robbery, driving while impaired, possession of narcotics, assault with a weapon and assaulting a police officer. What made that night's situation even worse, was that he was on the second day of a non-stop drinking binge.

Rusty, his older brother Randy Michell and two friends had been planning on going deer hunting Christmas Day and on the afternoon before, the four of them were drinking at sister Bonnie Michell's house. Bonnie lived 15 kilometres north of Lillooet on the Moha Road. Rusty was drifting in and out of consciousness, and the others were taunting him because he couldn't handle his liquor. The ridicule triggered his anger and suddenly, he left.

According to brother Randy, "He up and took off on us, he didn't really say anything." Given Michell's condition, it's not likely he could have said anything.

Although prohibited from driving, Michell had borrowed a friend's 1979 Oldsmobile. He drove home, south on the Moha Road back to the Bridge River Reserve and pulled into the driveway. His common-law wife Kathy James and the five Michell children were inside. Michell was not only raving drunk, he was also raging mad, and he ran up the back stairs and into the house totally out of control.

"He just started throwing stuff around." Kathy told RCMP operator Mills.

What Kathy James didn't say was that Rusty was so enraged he threw the kitchen table against the stove with such force it broke the tempered glass in the oven door. Then he threw a plate of food at Kathy, missing her and hitting the kitchen cupboard above the refrigerator.

At that point, Kathy James left the children and ran out into the night across the gravelled Indian reserve road to her aunt's house. There she placed the phone call to the RCMP.

Although Rusty had not been abusive to her in well over two years, his behavior that evening was particularly violent, and Kathy desperately feared for her safety. Even if Rusty left, she was convinced he would come back and beat her. She knew Rusty well enough to know that this night she needed police protection.

Telecoms operator Debbie Mills needed a lot of immediate information.

"Where's he at? Where do you live? Just give me some directions how to get to your house. You're at Bridge River, at six mile, do you have a house number?"

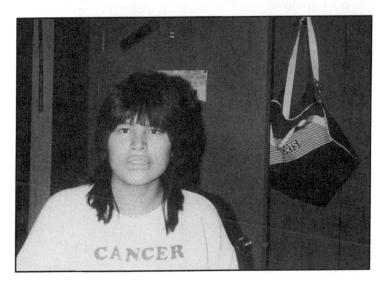

Top: *Kathy James's house, top - centre. The circular depressions of traditional pithouses can be seen in the foreground.*
Above: *Kathy James.*

By now Kathy was frantic. Michell was speeding away from their house. Her uncle said he thought he'd seen Rusty putting one of the children in the car.

"He's leaving in the car!" By now, Kathy was screaming into the phone.

Telecoms operator Mills had been trained to contain emotion. She needed details, not panic, if she was going to provide a quick RCMP response.

"OK, what's he driving?"

"A green four-door Oldsmobile."

"Did he hurt you at all, Kathy?"

"No."

The Bridge River Reserve where Rusty and Kathy lived is on benchland a hundred metres above the Bridge River. It's been the home of native Indians for centuries and where there are no modern houses, the land is still marked with the large circular outlines of the traditional pithouses. The one road in and out of the Bridge River Reserve climbs steeply up from the bench to the Moha Road. The Moha Road travels northwest from Lillooet parallel to the Bridge River.

Now looking through the window, from the safety of her aunt's house, Kathy could see Rusty Michell driving up to the Moha Road. Then suddenly, Michell stopped the car. He quickly spun around on the graveled road and headed back towards the house.

Still on the phone to Debbie Mills, Kathy screamed, "He's coming back towards the reserve. He's coming back down." The fear was obvious, Kathy was terrified.

Mills needed more information, calmly she asked, "OK Kathy, just tell me where your house is, OK?"

"It's a couple of miles past the bridge, in the new subdivision. It's a beige house."

Rusty Michell.

For Kathy James, the situation couldn't be worse. From her aunt's house, she could see the green Oldsmobile, its exhaust curling up in the below-zero temperature, the head lights shining on the side of her house. God, she thought, what's he doing now? Was he taking the children? Was he getting one of his rifles? Was he coming back to beat her? Although she didn't know what was going on Michell's mind, Kathy James knew she needed the RCMP.

Still keeping Kathy James on the telephone, Mills called the Lillooet RCMP detachment office on the RCMP radio. She reached Lillooet RCMP Constable Stan Walstrom, a four-year member of the Mounted Police. On Christmas Eve it's RCMP practice to have officers without children on duty. Being single, Walstrom was working the Christmas Eve shift.

Stan Walstrom was a status Indian and had been posted in Lillooet for three and a half years, his first assignment out of the RCMP Training depot in Regina.

Walstrom was a powerfully built young man and carried himself like a well-conditioned athlete. He also had an interesting background.

Stan Walstrom was born at the Prince George Regional Hospital, May 29, 1965. Before his birth, a decision had been made by the Ministry of Social Services and the Department of Indian Affairs officials that the infant would be placed with Elmer and Jennie Walstrom, white foster parents living in Ft. St. James. This placement was seen as being in the best interests of the baby, and the natural mother, who was from the Stellako Indian Reserve west of Prince George.

The Walstroms were well known as caring foster parents and they lovingly welcomed the new baby boy into their home. Stan Walstrom spent his first six years in Ft. St. James. Then Elmer Walstrom, who suffered badly from asthma, was told to move to a warmer climate. The Walstroms first moved to Comox on Vancouver Island and then to Lumby BC, a small community just east of Vernon in the North Okanagan. Stan Walstrom finished high school in Lumby and for the next few years was employed at local sawmills and construction sites. He also worked for a logging contractor in Mackenzie BC, 160 kilometres north of Prince George.

But Stan Walstrom was becoming increasingly interested in police work and ironically in the spring of 1989, went to Lillooet to learn more about the local native peacekeeper program. It was there that he heard the RCMP were looking for aboriginal recruits. With this knowledge, Stan applied to the RCMP and on August 23,

1989, Stan Walstrom signed his enlistment papers with the Mounted Police.

Force policy is to have native recruits spend two months in a predominantly native community to better understand the role of a police officer. The recruits ride around with RCMP officers, work at the detachment offices, review files and generally gain a first-hand understanding of police work. It's an orientation program that's proved to be invaluable, as many aspiring native police officers have found out that the "spit and polish" para-military regimen of the RCMP just isn't for them. But, Stan Walstrom who was sent back to Lillooet for the program, enjoyed his two-month preview of the RCMP and on October 11, 1989 went to the RCMP training depot in Regina for the six-month native officer program. On completion of the course he was sent back to Lillooet for the normal four-year RCMP posting.

When he first arrived in Lillooet, Stan Walstrom had a difficult time with his aboriginal background. He was a native Indian by birth, but not by upbringing. He was shocked at his naivety when it came to understanding the living conditions on Indian reservations. To compound the problem, the RCMP made Walstrom the Lillooet aboriginal affairs officer. Walstrom had grown up in white communities and had no idea of how to handle native issues. But, he persevered, taking the time to talk to the many natives he met in Lillooet and within two years he had earned the respect of the native community.

Stan Walstrom was also a quick study when it came to police procedure and policy. RCMP colleagues and superior officers considered Walstrom to be a good policeman. Later on that evening he'd call on everything he'd been taught.

When Debbie Mills called, Walstrom answered, "Lillooet. Go ahead."

Mills asked, "Do you know where Kathy James lives at Bridge River?"

"Kathy James?"

Kamloops is 140 kilometres in a direct line east from Lillooet and although the RCMP use radio repeater towers, communications signals are frequently bounced around and scrambled in the Lillooet valley.

Debbie Mills tried Walstrom again.

"You're coming in broken, but 10-4, you know where she lives? Beige house, new subdivision?"

Walstrom was still having trouble with the radio connection and asked for a repeat, saying, "I didn't catch the name, Kamloops, go again."

"Surname is James, given one is Kathy."

Walstrom heard it this time. "10-4, I've got it."

Kamloops Telecoms quickly briefed Walstrom on the situation, "OK apparently a Russell Michell came into her house, I can't find out if she — or I'm trying to find out if she lives with this guy — but he's 43 (a criminal-code numerical reference to heavy intoxication. Appendix A) he started trashing the house. He left the house, but now he's coming back. She's worried, she's got kids, small kids at the house."

"Oh shit," Stan Walstrom said to himself. Rusty Michell was absolutely the last person he wanted to hear about on what he had hoped would turn out to be a quiet Christmas Eve night shift.

Shortly after being posted to Lillooet in 1990, Stan Walstrom had seen Rusty Michell's violent side. The newly arrived rookie Mountie had arrested Michell at the downtown Lillooet Taxi stand on a charge of spousal abuse. It had been a difficult arrest for Stan Walstrom, but not an out-of-the-ordinary one when dealing with Rusty Michell. It took two officers, Stan Walstrom and Constable John Stringer to contain Michell and handcuff him.

Michell was never an easy arrest. Even with his hands cuffed behind him, he struggled with Stan Walstrom, they lost their footing and fell to the ground. On the way down Michell hit his head against the trunk lid of the police car, causing a deep cut above his eye.

The two police officers took Michell to the hospital, where, even handcuffed, he was so violent, the attending doctor couldn't stitch up the cut. So Stringer and Walstrom simply held Rusty down while the doctor applied a butterfly bandage. Then they transported him back to the RCMP lockup where he spent the night, sleeping off a big drunk, a sore head, and a lot of pent-up anger.

Michell next came to Walstrom's attention as part of his on-the-job orientation as a newly posted member of the RCMP. One element of RCMP recruit field-training policy is to have new members study the files of known criminals, particularly violent offenders, in order to better understand the nature of their behavior and know how to handle them should the need arise. Michell's file was one of Walstrom's "study" files, and it contained a long record of violence, spousal abuse, break and enter, narcotics possession and numerous weapons offences.

Walstrom was aware that Rusty Michell was a nasty son-of-a-bitch who was never brought in without a fight and now he was threatening his wife and children. Michell was obviously drunk, breaking up the house, no doubt beating up Kathy, and knowing his criminal record as he did, Walstrom had to assume Michell would be armed.

"He's taken my kids!" Kathy James was frantically yelling into the phone at Kamloops communications operator Debbie Mills.

"OK. Are you married to him?"

"Common-law."

Marital status was the last thing on Kathy's mind. Her children were in serious danger.

Again she screamed into the phone, "He's taken my kids. He's taken them all!"

"OK, how many kids have you got?"

"There's five of them."

Always calm, always cool, Debbie Mills needed Kathy to control herself, stay observant and stay on the phone. This was critical. At this point Kathy was the only one who could help the police keep on top of the situation.

"There's five kids? OK. Just hold on, he's on his way out there, but I just want to keep you on the line."

Telecoms quickly called back to Stan Walstrom.

"OK. Apparently he's gone back to the house, he's taken all five kids and he's just trying to leave right now. She's calling from a neighbor's house."

Stan Walstrom responded, "10-4 Kamloops. Now ask her which way he's going."

"Kathy?"

"Yes"

"Can you see which way they're going?" At that point Walstrom broke in again, he still needed more information. Mills continued: "Kathy, whose house are you at? He needs to know whose house you're at?"

"I'm at my aunt's house."

That meant nothing to Walstrom and he asked Mills to get Kathy's phone number so he could talk to her first hand.

"OK. What's the phone number you're at. He wants to talk to you right away, OK, so you're gonna have to give me the number.

"It's 7-3-7-6"

Mills repeated the number. "7376? OK. Hang up and he's going to phone you, right away, OK? Bye-bye."

"Alpha Three, Kathy's number is 7376"

Immediately, Walstrom picked up the phone and called Kathy James from the RCMP detachment. It was obvious from the frantic conversation that she was terrified. She described to him how Rusty had come home, yelling and swearing and throwing things around. She needed police assistance immediately. Walstrom remembered the many times he'd seen Kathy James's bruised and swollen face from beatings she'd taken from Michell. This call was no hoax. If Kathy James said she was in serious trouble, she meant it.

Stan Walstrom needed backup. RCMP policy is to treat all complaints of spousal abuse as a criminal matter. Regulations advise that violence in relationships constitutes a high risk to the responding officer. There was no way Walstrom was going after a drunk Rusty Michell on his own. Michell was just too nasty, too tough, and on this night, clearly out of control.

There are two police forces in Lillooet. The RCMP, and since 1991, the Stl'At'Lmx Nation Tribal Police. For ease of pronunciation, the native police force is generally referred to as the STNP. It was the first native police force established in British Columbia and is located on the Lillooet Band reserve off Rancherie Drive south of Lillooet on a large flat field of land overlooking the town.

That night, STNP Constable Keith McKay was on duty. McKay was one of seven officers in the force and had re-

Top: *Stan Walstrom.*
Above: *Keith McKay.*

ceived his provincial government appointment as a Special Constable just a week earlier. But in spite of the recent appointment, McKay was no rookie. In 1988 he had started training in Lillooet as a native peace keeper, which meant he had the authority of a peace officer but only on the Stl'At'Lmx Reserve.

In 1990 McKay was accepted to the Native Justice Institute at Mission, BC, for police officer training. It's a ten month course, taught by instructors from the BC Justice Institute, and is the same course of studies taken by members of British Columbia's municipal police forces. Following the Native Justice Institute program, Keith McKay did a two-month practicum with the Sioux Valley, Manitoba native police force. He returned to Lillooet to work as a peace keeper and was later taken on as a police officer with the STNP.

Keith McKay, a bright, self-assured young man, looked considerably younger than his twenty-six years. But behind the apparent youthfulness was a solid temperament and maturity. Following Walstrom's call to Kathy James, he phoned the STNP detachment, the call was forwarded to Keith McKay. Walstrom quickly briefed McKay on the incident taking place at the Bridge River Reserve and asked him to assist in the response.

As it happened, McKay had dropped in that Christmas Eve night to visit with a friend who lived on Lillooet's Main Street across from the British Columbia Rail station. It took McKay just minutes to drive the few kilometres down Main Street to the RCMP detachment where Stan Walstrom was waiting in police car Twenty-Two Alpha Three. Keith McKay parked his STNP Ford Explorer in the RCMP lot, got in the passenger seat of the

RCMP Chevrolet Caprice. Then the two officers sped north out of town to the Bridge River Reserve.

At this point, Telecoms operator Madeline Riley took over for Debbie Mills. Mills was the city detachment operator and had the only open telephone line at the time when the call had come in from Kathy James. Madeline Riley, one of the two communications operators assigned to cover the rural Kamloops subdivision, would be the RCMP communications lifeline to the responding police officers for the rest of the long and troubled evening.

Riley continued briefing Walstrom with an updated identification of Rusty Michell. "Yeah. Twenty-Two Alpha Three. Not sure if you're familiar with this Russell Michell. He's on Lillooet entry, prohib firearms, CNI 10-80, 82, FTA on driving."

In civilian language, that meant Rusty Michell had a record of violence, a record of carrying offensive weapons and he was prohibited from driving due to a string of impaired convictions dating back to 1982.

"Sounds like a real charming guy." Keith McKay said to Stan.

Walstrom responded, covering off his concern with an attempt at some humor. "You got it. Let me tell you, Rusty Michell is trouble, big trouble. Merry Christmas, Constable McKay."

Within minutes of Kathy James's phone call to the RCMP, Walstrom and McKay came upon Michell and the green 1979 Oldsmobile 88. He was twelve kilometres north of Lillooet on the Moha Road, speeding south. Walstrom was heading north and as soon as he saw the green Oldsmobile pass him, he did an immediate U-turn and began the pursuit.

Top: *The beginning of West Pavilion Road.*
Above: *West Pavilion Road cuts into the steep side hills.*

As soon as Michell saw the police car slow, change direction and turn to follow him, he started evasive action. Two hundred metres south on the Moha Road from the point where Walstrom and McKay first saw Michell, the West Pavilion logging road takes off to the left. Michell took the turn as fast as he could, tires spinning on the gravel road, headlights shining at the rocky hills on one side and over the dark emptiness on the other. He had seen the police car do its quick turn on the Moha Road and there was no doubt they were after him.

Michell knew the West Pavilion Road well; he'd often gone night hunting there for mule deer. But tonight, Christmas Eve 1993, would be more than just another night hunt. Michell's next two hours that evening would be a snapshot of his life; boozy, on the verge of arrest, and violent.

The West Pavilion Road is a narrow logging road, hanging precariously on the steep West Pavilion side hills. For the most part it is just two vehicle-widths wide, but at times it narrows to one lane only. There are no guard rails, no shoulders, no warning signs, only unmarked switchbacks and the icy Fraser River flowing hundreds of metres below. That evening, the West Pavilion logging road was a narrow, dangerous track covered in glare ice.

RCMP procedure during a hazardous pursuit calls for the officers involved to maintain constant contact with the RCMP Communications Centre. As soon as Stan Walstrom turned to follow Michell, he called in: "Kamloops, we've got the subject in the four-door Oldsmobile, and we're going up West Pavilion Road, no chase as of yet. However, we're approaching him and we're about to activate our lights. If you can note that please."

Fourteen minutes after Kathy James's call to the RCMP, Stan Walstrom hit the dash-mounted toggle switches for the police car's emergency equipment lights, and he and Keith McKay began a code-three pursuit up the icy West Pavilion Road. Russell Michell had to be stopped and apprehended.

3

POLICE FORCES IN NORTH AMERICA prefer full-size, rear-wheel drive cars for general-duty police work. There are only two manufacturers who still build cars to these requirements. Ford with the Crown Victoria Police Interceptor and General Motors with the Chevrolet Caprice Police Standard. Unlike the specially-optioned high-speed pursuit cars of the 1960s, today's full-size police cars use standard equipment motors and are built more for heavy-duty service than high-speed pursuits. Police forces, including the RCMP, who need fast cars for highway patrol duty buy high-powered V-8 sport coupes such as the Ford Mustang and Chevrolet Camaro.

The major differences between standard-size police cars and the civilian models are the former's heavy-duty motor and transmission cooling systems, valve-train durability features, hard-service brakes and brake linings, as well as special electrical systems, and strengthened police-service perimeter frames in anticipation of high-speed bumping or use of the car as a barricade.

The most noticeable performance changes on current police cars are the front and rear suspension systems. Police cars have massive front and rear stabilizer bars, heavy-duty shock absorbers and stiffer coil-spring rates to keep the car rock-solid and stable under all driving conditions. These modifications allow for absolutely flat cornering during high-speed maneuvers. It's truly a "point-and-go" suspension set up, designed to instill driver confidence during fast and dangerous hazardous pursuits.

The RCMP cars in Lillooet were Chevrolet Caprices; they had 5.0 litre motors, were fitted with snow tires and were well suited for rural rough-road police duty.

In spite of the flashing police car lights, it was clear that Rusty Michell had no intentions of stopping for Constables Stan Walstrom and Keith McKay as they followed him in PC Twenty-Two Alpha Three, a blue and white 1993 Police Standard Chevrolet Caprice.

The first part of the West Pavilion Road that evening was good compacted gravel, and on the straight stretches between the hair pin corners, Rusty Michell attempted to put some distance between himself and the pursuing police car.

The Kamloops radio transmission crackled over the mountaintop repeater towers to Police Car Twenty-Two Alpha Three. At that point, Telecoms operator Riley, repeated Michell's police record entries to Stan Walstrom, "Just to advise, the suspect is a prohibited driver."

Brevity and politeness are the rules of police radio conversations, Stan Walstrom was well aware of Rusty Michell's prohibited-driver status from the hours he'd spent going over Michell's lengthy criminal record. But, he wasn't aware that Madeline Riley was now handling communications. Stan Walstrom was clearly on edge; his answer was less than polite.

"10-4. I'm aware of that. That's why we're going after him."

It was clear the tension was mounting. Walstrom, realizing that the Telecoms operator was only doing her job, added, "I just can't catch up to him."

RCMP mountaintop radio repeaters are battery operated and to save on battery life, are set to shut down automatically after being on for three minutes. When this automatic shutdown happens, it can take as long as thirty seconds for the remote repeater to be activated again. The communications operator can also shut the repeater down from the Telecoms console. When an operator-controlled shutdown occurs, there is no delay in re-activating the repeater and the next communications between the police car and the Telecoms centre begins immediately.

Madeline Riley wanted an immediate call from Stan Walstrom when he was about to stop Rusty Michell. She also had a pretty cheery outlook on the status of the pursuit and assumed it would end quickly. She called Stan Walstrom: "10-4. I don't want the repeater to fall, so just call me when you're going to stop him."

Walstrom called back, "10-4. We're about three vehicle-lengths behind him now and we're just gonna start the siren here, you wanna copy."

"Go ahead."

Next, Stan Walstrom called Madeline Riley for a motor vehicle identification check. "The plates are Alpha Charlie Echo, 6-3-4. (Appendix B) He's not responding to the dome lights, to the wig wags and the siren."

"You're how far west?"

"Yeah, we're approximately three kilometres on the West Pavilion Road. He's just driving and he's ignoring us."

"Not speeding though?"

"No. Now we're at the 12 kilometre mark on West Pavilion Road, just passed it.

Industrial logging roads are marked every kilometre with a distance sign. Because of the many blind corners and the inability of a loaded logging truck to stop or maneuver quickly around oncoming vehicles, traffic must be radio controlled.

During the working hours when logging trucks are on the road, all vehicles use CB radios on a pre-determined channel to call out the kilometre sign they've just passed. Going into a logging site, when the trucks would be un-loaded, the radio protocol is, "Vehicle at kilometre 12 — empty." Going out it's, " Vehicle at kilometre 12 — loaded." This lets all other traffic know where you are, and more importantly, which direction you're travelling.

However, logging road communications protocol would not be needed that lonely Christmas Eve night as police car Twenty-Two Alpha Three, with Stan Walstrom and Keith McKay inside, followed Rusty Michell up the twisting glare-ice road into the West Pavilion hills.

RCMP Sergeant Al Olsen would be the fourth man up the West Pavilion Road that evening. When Walstrom and McKay had started the pursuit, Kamloops Telecoms had called Olsen to advise him of the unfolding events. Olsen, the Non-commissioned Officer in charge of the RCMP Lillooet detachment, was at home that evening wrapping Christmas presents for his two boys.

Al Olsen.

He had rented a video, and he and his wife Joan were having a drink and looking forward to a quiet Christmas Eve at home with the family.

Al Olsen was a twenty-year veteran of the force. Originally from Bawlf, Alberta, he had gone through the RCMP training depot in Regina. In August 1973, he began his rookie stint in the predominantly native community of Alexis Creek, British Columbia. Olsen was a big, tough, no-nonsense policeman. More importantly, he had good instincts. In the last five years of his career he had distinguished himself as a smart, common-sense investigator with a ready ability to take charge in difficult situations.

Al Olsen's career path was typical for a member of the force serving in British Columbia. Following his first posting in Alexis Creek, Al Olsen was assigned to the Kelowna RCMP detachment. It was in 1979 in Kelowna where he met his wife-to-be Joan. They were married in Kelowna and had two boys, Brad and Chad.

Following several postings in the BC southern Interior, Constable Al Olsen was assigned in 1988 to the Vancouver Island community of Sidney. It was there that his investigative skills and determination would result in a significant set of arrests following a particularly horrifying crime.

On October 12, 1988, Al Olsen, then still at the Constable rank, was working the midnight watch. At 6:15 that morning he was called to the Saanich Peninsula Twasout Indian Reserve. He came on a brutal scene. Sixty-six-year-old Sidney cab driver Kenneth Scott was dead in the front seat of his taxi with numerous stab wounds to his neck and chest. Scott was a retired Texaco refinery production worker who had worked in Trinadad for several years before retiring to Sidney BC to join the Sidney-based Beacon Cab company as an owner-operator with a share in the company. Scott's death left behind his wife Marlene and four adult children.

RCMP Sergeant Jim Peters assigned Al Olsen to the "file," the RCMP term signifying Olsen would be in charge of the Kenneth Scott murder investigation. Olsen began scouring the heavily wooded murder scene for evidence. At 9:00 a.m. while still at the Sidney Twasout Reserve, he learned over his police car radio that only a few kilometres away, Central Saanich Municipal Police had picked up three native lads on the Keating Cross Road in Sannich. They had all been drinking heavily and had assaulted a fifteen year old boy on his way to school. The boy had been kicked repeatedly in the stomach and had a black eye from the beating.

Immediately, Al Olsen contacted the Saanich police telling them to hold the boys until he got there. When Olsen arrived, he searched the boys and on one of them found a blood-stained knife. After extensive questioning by Al Olsen, the tragic events of the Scott murder came out. The boys admitted to Olsen that they had been drinking all night and had planned to kill somebody before the evening was over.

As they recounted the events of that morning, Olsen was sickened by the senselessness of the crime. Shortly before 5:30 a.m. the native lads had hailed Scott's cab in the Brentwood Bay area and asked to be taken back to the Twasout Reserve. Once on the reserve they told Scott to stop the cab. It was a heavily treed area and at that time of the morning there was no other traffic. They demanded cash from Scott and when he refused, one of the boys hit Scott in the head with the butt of a pellet gun, then drew a combat-style knife and stabbed the elderly cab driver repeatedly in the neck and chest.

Under further questioning from Constable Olsen, the boys continued to describe the grisly events of their early-morning killing spree. They told Olsen how Scott had lost consciousness following the blow to the head and the knife attack. Having previously put a case of beer in the trunk of the taxi, they calmly got out of the cab, walked to the back, opened the trunk and each had a beer. Then one of the boys went back to the driver's seat of the cab and savagely stabbed Ken Scott several more times. It was a brutal, pointless killing.

By midday, the boys had provided Al Olsen with enough information to arrest the fourth member in on the killing at his home. As it turned out, two of the boys were from Duncan BC, and two were from the Tsawout Reserve at Sidney. Olsen now had all the evidence he needed and the boys were charged. Only one, twenty-three year-old Michael Lee Allen, was tried publicly. A year later, on October 4, 1989 and after eight hours of deliberation, a Supreme Court jury found Allen guilty of manslaughter, although the prosecution had asked for a conviction of first-degree murder, the jury returned the lesser verdict. Michael Allen received a four-year sentence and was eligible for parole in eight months.

The three other boys, all minors and under the protection of the Young Offenders Act, were not tried in adult court and neither their names, nor their sentences or release dates from the juvenile detention unit were ever revealed.

The RCMP liked the determined attitude that Al Olsen had shown in the Scott murder investigation. In the fall of 1989, Al Olsen was offered and accepted a promotion to corporal, a raise in salary and a posting in Fort St. James, 160 kilometres northwest of Prince George. There, as one of two RCMP corporals with seven constables under him, Olsen became heavily involved in community relations and soon established a well-deserved reputation as the type of policeman who could deal fairly and objectively with the native community and its many problems. Al Olsen had worked hard to earn the trust of the native leaders and his efforts had paid off.

But it was in Fort St. James where another tragic event would shape his career, hone his skills as a take-charge police officer, yet leave him with deep emotional scars.

On February 19, 1991, a few minutes before midnight, the RCMP in Fort St. James received a call for help from the Pinchie Indian Reserve. The reserve is 40 kilometres north of Fort St. James and is located on the east side of Stuart Lake.

Randy John Monk, a twenty-four year-old native living on the Pinchie Reserve had been drinking heavily in Fort St. James that evening. He returned to Pinchie with three six-packs of beer. There he continued to drink at the reserve home of his friends Stan and Alex Tom.

Randy, a nephew of Carrier Sekani Tribal Chief Justa Monk, was sadly typical of so many of the troubled youth who live on Indian reserves. When sober, Randy was known to friends, as well as by the RCMP, as a nice enough fellow, but when he drank there was a destructive and violent side to his behavior. Because of this, Monk was on the waiting list for admission to a native-run substance-abuse program.

Up until a week before the February 19 call, Randy, his pregnant common-law wife Christal Murdoch and their three children, had been living with Christal's parents at the Murdoch home on the Pinchie Reserve. But Randy's constant drinking had been too much for the family. He'd been ordered out of the house and told to fend for himself. It was a sad and humiliating situation for Randy. He couldn't support his wife and family and since decent housing was not available, he had nowhere to live. For comfort he compounded his problem by turning again to alcohol.

After drinking with Stan and Alex Tom, Randy made his way as best he could down the street to the Murdoch home. Christal's parents were out for the evening and Christal let him in. Randy was loud, drunk and ready to pick a fight, after fifteen minutes Christal made him leave. Randy stumbled down the road and broke into a house a few doors away from the Murdoch home. The owner was away that evening, Randy found a .308 caliber hunting rifle and some loose rifle shells. Then he called his mother, who also lived on the reserve, and threatened to commit suicide. He morbidly asserted that he was going to join his father who had been killed in a shoot out with the RCMP years earlier.

It was a desperate plea for help, and in Monk's own boozy way he attempted to reinforce his despondency by working the bolt action of the .308 rifle so his mother could hear it over the phone.

Following the phone conversation, Randy left the house and proceeded down the reserve road to threatening and confronting the neighbors. It was then that his mother, genuinely believing the suicide threats, called the police.

Corporal Al Olsen responded with RCMP Constable Hayley Reid, a native member of the RCMP from Burns Lake and a new recruit in the native policing program. Olsen and Reid quickly drove the 40 kilometres to the Pinchie Village, arriving at 12:45 in the morning. They cruised through the village in their RCMP GMC Suburban 4X4.

Al Olsen couldn't spot Monk, but he quickly realized the village street lighting made them sitting targets and he drove the blue-and- white Suburban back out to the road leading into the village.

They parked on the outer reserve road and waited. In the mean time, Monk's behavior was becoming more erratic. He returned to the empty house and called the RCMP. He repeated his suicide threats, saying he had a gun to his head and began demanding to speak to Constable Mike Brooks. Brooks was another native member of the RCMP and Monk no doubt thought Brooks could offer him a sympathetic ear. At 1:16, Monk called the RCMP again, with more threats. During this conversation, the BC Telephone company was able to trace the call to the home of Francis Dennis.

Olsen and Reid stayed on the outer reserve road, 100 metres away from the village. Al Olsen, no rookie, realized that he and Reid could be easily shot by Monk if they entered the village. Monk was armed with a rifle, drunk and bent on suicide or murder. He also had the advantage of being able to shoot from the cover of the trees or the shadows of any of the Pinchie Reserve homes. With this concern in mind, Olsen called for backup from the Fort St. James RCMP detachment and instructed the responding members to bring rifles with them.

Constables Hugh Malone and Pat Slawter responded, setting out for the Pinchie Reserve at 2:56 AM. In addition to their .38 Smith and Wesson Police Special revolvers and the Remington 12-gauge pump shotgun carried in all RCMP vehicles, Malone and Slawter were both armed with two RCMP-issue Winchester Model 70 .308 rifles.

Monk continued to lurch from door to door in the Pinchie village. He returned to the Dennis home and between 2:00 and 2:30 that winter morning made three phone calls to the Murdochs. During one of those calls he said he wanted a "shoot out" with the RCMP.

At 3:02 a.m. Monk's mother-in-law, Peggy Murdoch, called the RCMP to say she'd heard a rifle shot. This message was immediately relayed to Al Olsen, still parked on the road into the Pinchie Reserve, who confirmed he too had heard a shot. But, Olsen also knew that Monk had a habit of passing out and sleeping off his drinking bouts. He figured the best plan was to leave the Pinchie Village and return to Fort St. James. The police did not have control of the situation, and Al Olsen knew he would be putting himself and the other members at considerable risk if they attempted to search for Randy Monk in the dark.

Olsen also figured that even if Monk had shot himself it would be futile and still potentially dangerous to look for him in the dark. Plus, the weather was unseasonably warm for February, well above the freezing level during the day, with just a few degrees of frost at night. There was little risk of Randy Monk suffering from exposure. Olsen, called Slawter and Malone on the police radios, and told them to return to Ft. St. James. Then he shifted the idling Suburban into gear and he and Haley Reid began the drive back to Ft. St. James.

However, Randy Monk had not shot himself, he was not giving up, and he was not about to pass out. At 3:32 in the morning, Randy's mother-in-law Peggy Murdoch, phoned the RCMP to say Randy was back at their home, he was attempting to break in, he had a rifle and was acting in such a violent manner that Peggy had the whole family huddled away from the windows and on the floor in the hallway.

This message was quickly passed on to Al Olsen. Hearing this, he knew he had to take control of the situation. The Pinchie villagers were at serious risk. Monk was becoming increasingly violent and had to be disarmed and arrested before he took his life or killed someone. When the call from Peggy Murdoch came, Olsen, Reid, Malone and Slawter were just arriving back at Ft. St. James. On Olsen's instructions, the RCMP officers quickly turned around and headed back on the snow-covered 40 kilometre road to the Pinchie Reserve.

While the two RCMP Suburbans were speeding back to Pinchie, Randy Monk's behavior was becoming more and more irrational. He returned to the Murdoch home, banged on the locked front door and threatened to kill Christal's father Philip Murdoch. Desperately fearing for his life and that of his family, Murdoch grabbed his .22 caliber rifle and fired at Monk through the window of the front door. The bullet hit Monk in the side of his right arm a few inches below the shoulder. The small-caliber bullet, lacking the velocity to exit the body, travelled laterally just under the surface of the skin and finally lodged in the soft flesh of Monk's right pectoral muscle. The wound itself was not life threatening. Indeed, given Monk's intoxicated condition, it's not likely he would have felt much more than a momentary sting from the .22 caliber round.

Peggy Murdoch was still on the phone to the RCMP, she told them her husband had just shot Randy Monk. The RCMP officer advised her the four officers were on their way back to the village and an ambulance was being dispatched to Pinchie from Fort St. James.

Following the shot, Monk bolted from the Murdoch front door. He ran for cover behind one of the reserve homes. Though the small-caliber bullet wound was not in any way disabling, he fell repeatedly, bruising his face, scratching his hands, and scraping his shin and right knee.

As the four RCMP members arrived back at the reserve, Al Olsen, the senior officer, stopped both police vehicles on the road leading into the reserve. There he discussed with the other three officers how they were going to handle Randy Monk, should he become violent or aggressive.

It was a tense situation and they knew it. The police were on reserve land. Monk, though drunk and threatening to kill, was with his own people and some of the villagers would view the police as trespassers. Olsen made the decision that he and fourteen-year RCMP veteran

Constable Hugh Malone would be armed with the Winchester .308 rifles and approach the Murdoch home located at the end of the reserve road. It was there they believed Randy Monk was hiding in the shadows of the house.

Constable Pat Slawter would be armed with the Remington 12-gauge pump-action shotgun and take up a position behind the row of reserve homes in the event that Monk attempted to escape into the wooded area in back of the houses. Constable Hayley Reid would stay in the police car and maintain radio contact.

Calmly, Al Olsen instructed the members that "deadly force" would be used if necessary. On the RCMP continuum of increasing levels of force to be used in threatening situations, deadly force is the last stage and is coldly and clinically used to describe any situation "where the officer fears grievous bodily harm or death, whether the suspect is armed or not." The deadly-force procedure is: warn, draw, point, fire.

Al Olsen went through the conditions where deadly force would be used. If Monk attempted to enter the Murdoch home; if he was warned to drop his rifle, but didn't; if he began shooting or threatened to shoot. If any of these events occurred, he was to be brought down.

Olsen concluded his instructions to the other three with the observation that there seemed to be little chance of the RCMP taking control of the situation without engaging in a shoot out with Randy Monk. Then, Olsen and Malone moved quietly on the reserve road down to the home of Francis Dennis. There was a street light in front of the house and they proceeded slowly trying to stay in the shadows of the village buildings.

A one-metre-wide metal culvert lay on the ground in front of the Dennis door. The culvert would provide some cover for Malone and Olsen. From their vantage point they saw Monk move out from the shadows of the Murdoch home, about 80 metres away. But had he seen them? He was acting strangely. He'd move out into the light and then quickly back again into the shadows on the side of the Murdoch house. At all times carrying his rifle in both hands, ready to fire.

The last thing Al Olsen wanted, was to lose sight of Randy Monk in the native village. If he lost sight of Monk it meant he had lost control of the situation. Monk could easily slip around the back of the Murdoch home and come up behind the police officers, or he could move farther away and shoot at them from the cover of the trees. Al Olsen told fellow officer Hugh Malone to stay at the front of the Dennis residence, while he moved around back to tell Constable Pat Slawter that Monk may attempt to come around behind them.

Suddenly, Monk appeared at the front side of the Murdoch house. He was in plain view of Hugh Malone. Monk came toward Malone, then quickly raised his rifle, pointing it directly at the RCMP officer.

A Winchester Model 70 .308 is a popular hunting rifle and effective for shooting deer, antelope and black bear. It's also widely used by law enforcement and military sharpshooters. A .308 with a standard 150 grain hunting cartridge has a muzzle velocity of 2820 feet per second. The force of the bullet at the muzzle is measured at 2648 pounds of energy. At a distance of 80 meters, the velocity will drop marginally to 2559 feet per second, the energy to 2061 foot pounds. But a .308 round has such deadly stopping power that at well over the length of three football fields, it easily penetrates skin, bone and muscle. At that distance, one well-placed shot from a .308 will drop a full-grown moose, or man, instantly.

Monk took one more step towards Hugh Malone. A shot rang out. The high velocity cracking sound splitting the air, echoing through the village and over the ice on the nearby Stuart Lake. A bright orange muzzle flash spit out of the rifle barrel. Monk, right handed, had his rifle pulled tight to his right shoulder. His left arm was up, roughly parallel to the ground, elbow slightly bent as he held the stock of the rifle with his left hand, taking aim at Constable Hugh Malone. Randy Monk's right hand was around the grip, with his index finger on the trigger.

Malone's first shot tore into Monk's raised left arm, entering the forearm a few inches below the elbow. A ton of focused energy shattered the ulna and the radius, the bones of the lower arm. The bullet destroyed the elbow joint, and caused a massive fracture of the humerus, the bone of the upper arm. It was a straight-through shot. The bullet exited through muscle and skin of the left upper arm, a few inches above the elbow.

Immediately, Al Olsen ran back out into the street, and well past Hugh Malone, his rifle ready to fire. If he had to shoot at Monk, he didn't want to deafen Malone. Both Malone and Olsen screamed at Monk to drop his rifle, but Monk took another step forward, his shattered left arm now hanging uselessly at his side. But amazingly, and in spite of the massive wound to his left arm he was still managing to keep the rifle raised with his right hand.

Hugh Malone quickly fired again. His second shot hit Randy Monk a few inches above and to the right of the navel. The bullet passed through the abdominal wall, perforated the transverse colon and the vena cava, the main vein returning blood from the lower body to the heart. It was a massive wound to the gut. Monk collapsed on the ground, his rifle fell behind him. Olsen yelled at Malone to stay put and cover him, and then he quickly ran to the fallen man.

Olsen didn't know it, but in minutes, Randy Monk would be dead, as blood began to pump from the large perforated vein and pool in the abdominal cavity. Randy Monk was laying on his stomach. Al Olsen rolled him over, he opened Monk's shirt to check for vital signs. He could clearly see the entrance wound and Monk's stomach swelling from the massive internal bleeding.

He checked Randy Monk's rifle. "Fuck," Olsen swore quietly to himself. Monk's gun was empty! A few rifle shells had fallen out of Monk's pocket on to the ground, but they were later found to be 30.30 caliber rounds and could not have been fired in the .308 rifle he was carrying. Later Al Olsen would say, "Randy Monk committed suicide, he just got us to pull the trigger."

Hugh Malone was visibly shaken. Olsen took Hugh Malone's rifle, standard RCMP procedure following a shooting, and asked Malone if was capable of driving back to Fort St. James. Malone felt he could manage the trip and returned to town.

The ambulance, which had been waiting at the entrance road to the reserve was called in, Randy Monk was put on a stretcher, loaded in the ambulance and transported to Fort St. James. Hayley Reid went with the ambulance. The autopsy, completed two days later by forensic pathologist Dr. Jennifer Rice at the Prince George Regional Hospital, showed three litres of blood in the abdominal cavity. Randy Monk had probably died as the ambulance was leaving the Pinchie Reserve. The autopsy also revealed a blood alcohol content of 0.3 percent.

Hugh Malone was devastated by Monk's death. So was Al Olsen. Although he hadn't pulled the trigger, Olsen had given the orders to shoot to kill. An unarmed man was dead at their hand. Randy John Monk, a poor, drunk, tragic figure. No hope, no future and now dead.

The popular Hollywood notion that police officers have some sort of Dirty Harry "Make my day" attitude about taking the life of another human being is a cruel distortion and in no way reflects the personal agony police officers go through when they've been involved in a fatal shooting.

Following the shooting of Randy Monk the mood in the Fort St. James native community quickly turned ugly. Randy Monk was one of their own. The police had come in to their village and shot him. Monk's rifle was empty, and even if it would have loaded, could Monk in his drunken state have fired it with any accuracy? And why did the police come back a second time? Clearly, there were a lot of questions to be answered.

From April 29 to May 1, 1991, a coroner's inquest was held into the death of Randy Monk. Because of the serious questions surrounding Monk's death, BC Chief Coroner Vince Cain, a twenty-five-year former member of the RCMP, presided at the inquest. At Vince Cain's suggestion, the inquest was held at the community hall on the Tachie Reserve, just north of the Pinchie Village. Cain was of the opinion that if the Canadian justice system was going to dispense law and order on native reserves, then it was going to answer for its actions on native reserves.

It was a revealing inquest. As the evidence was presented, emotions ranged from anger to frustration to tears.

Corporal Al Olsen and Constable Hugh Malone had known Randy Monk personally. During their testimony, they both broke down and openly wept when they recalled the events that led to the shooting of Randy Monk. The Pinchie Villagers had not expected to see two seasoned white police officers in tears over the seemingly senseless shooting of a young man. And, as so often happens when tragic events are recounted, the inquest presented an opportunity for healing. Following the inquest, Randy Monk's mother went over to Al Olsen and hugged him. She clearly understood the tragic impact her son's death had had on even an experienced RCMP officer like Corporal Olsen. Little did Al Olsen know that within three years he would once again be caught up in similar tragic set of circumstances.

The Jury's verdict classified Monk's death as homicide. In the precise language of the Coroner's Court, "homicide" is explained as follows: it is a neutral term used to classify a death resulted from injuries caused directly or indirectly by the actions of another person without imputing blame or fault to that person.

In the spring of 1992, Al Olsen was promoted to the rank of sergeant, with a raise in pay. In the normal RCMP promotion schedule, it would have taken Al Olsen four years to make Sergeant. He did it in three and was appointed officer in charge of the Lillooet RCMP detachment.

Now thirty-two months later and 800 kilometres away from the Pinchie Indian Reserve, Sergeant Al Olsen was again being drawn into a potentially life-threatening situation. With so many members off duty that Christmas Eve,

Al Olsen had instructed the RCMP Kamloops Subdivision Telecoms centre that he was to be advised of any incidents of a serious nature. As soon as the communications centre contacted Olsen, described the circumstances facing Walstrom and McKay and provided the record on Rusty Michell, Olsen knew the two young officers needed backup.

Olsen was advised by Telecoms operator Riley that Michell had a record of violence, including spousal abuse and that he could have one or more children with him. Olsen also knew that at least 100 people lived between Lillooet and the Big Bar Ferry on the West Pavilion Road, so there was good reason to believe that if Michell was not apprehended, he would break into a home along the road or return to the Bridge River Reserve. Given his record of wife-beating, Kathy James would be at considerable risk if Michell returned. Al Olsen dressed quickly in the familiar grey-khaki shirt and dark-blue-pant field uniform of the RCMP.

"Shit," Olsen swore. He had left his .38 Smith and Wesson Police Special revolver in town at the RCMP detachment. It's a common procedure among senior police officers who have administrative duties and would not normally be on call to leave their sidearms locked up in their office desks.

Back on the West Pavilion Road, now only fifteen minutes after Kathy James's panic-stricken phone call to the RCMP, Police Constables Walstrom and McKay in their Chevrolet Caprice, were closely following Rusty Michell, their pulses quickening, although the police car's lights were flashing, and the siren was on, Stan Walstrom wasn't making any overt attempts on the snowy hill-side road, to force Michell over.

Walstrom called into Telecoms: "He's trying to take off a bit here, not really doing anything rambunctious though."

Telecoms responded, "10-4."

The emergency equipment on RCMP police cars provides a rolling light show, designed to see, and be seen. Centered between the familiar rotating blue and red lights, are bright white "takedown" lights. They're as bright and strong as high beams. To this array are added the "wig-wags," a special wiring unit that causes the police car's high-beams to flash alternatively from one side to the other.

With the police car's emergency equipment on, and with the reflection from the snowy road and side hills lighting up the night, Walstrom and McKay were easily able to see inside the swerving and skidding car ahead of them. Walstrom called into the RCMP Telecoms Centre: "He's wearing a blue ball cap, but can't visually identify him yet."

Short distance police car pursuits are common place, police officers handle them with ease. The siren goes on, the lights flash and the offending driver pulls over. However, when it becomes clear that the suspect being pursued is not going to stop, an adrenaline build up sets in. As the length of the chase increases, so does the tension. It's a natural reaction that happens in even the most seasoned officers.

That tension was beginning to mount in PC Twenty-Two Alpha Three. Stan Walstrom knew Rusty Michell was going to be a tough arrest, he risked a quick look at Keith McKay and said, "This guy is really out of it tonight, we've got a big problem on our hands." Then Walstrom called back to Telecoms, "Kamloops, we're doing approximately 70 kilometres an hour on a gravel road here."

This was no mean feat given the extremely icy driving conditions, on the dangerous mountainside road where, had Walstrom been able to look down to the right, he would have seen the steep, rock-covered drop falling 200 meters straight down to the cold Fraser River. Later, RCMP Corporal Fred Pearson, a senior member of the Lillooet detachment would joke and say, "If it had've been daytime, and Walstrom could've looked over the bank, he'd have crapped his pants."

It was a strange parade. First came the skidding Oldsmobile, driven as fast as its befuddled driver could manage, yet unable to put any distance between itself and the pursuing police car. Then came PC Twenty-Two Alpha Three, hanging in behind, all lights flashing, alternating fingers of blue/red lines sweeping across the Ponderosa pines and sagebrush on the steep snow-covered hill side.

Following Stan Walstrom's request for the license plate copy, communications operator Riley responded: "10-4. Alpha Three, Kamloops, that vehicle belongs to Roger Lazore, from the Pavilion Reserve."

"10-4 Kamloops. We just passed the 14 kilometre mark, he's still not stopping. We're not pursuing him an aggressive manner, we're just following with lights on, basically." RCMP regulations require a senior NCO to monitor a hazardous pursuit. Walstrom made the request. "You wanna contact watch commander and advise him of the same, please?"

RCMP Telecoms operator Madeline Riley had been a step ahead of Walstrom. "10-4. Watch commander's plugged in, right now.

At 20:01 hours, just 19 minutes after Kathy James had placed her frantic phone call, the pursuit was taking on a threatening momentum as Rusty Michell showed no signs of stopping.

Walstrom called again; he was getting nervous. "Kamloops, we've just passed the 16 kilometre mark, we're still following the subject and he's still ignoring us, no identification of the driver confirmed as yet, must be Michell, we'll keep you posted."

A minute later, the big Oldsmobile skidded completely sideways, its rear tires dangerously close to the edge, it recovered and straightened out. While in the skid, the car had been sideways long enough in the police cruiser's piercing takedown lights for Stan Walstrom to clearly see the side of Rusty Michell's face and make a positive identification.

"Well like it or not, we got the right guy, sure as hell, that's Rusty Michell," Walstrom said to Keith McKay. Then he called into Telecoms, "Kamloops, confirm it's Rusty Michell driving the vehicle. He just swerved the vehicle. It's Rusty Michell driving the vehicle. We have visual confirmation."

4

THE RCMP TELECOMS CENTRE serving both the Kamloops Subdivision and the City detachments is located in the RCMP City headquarters at the corner of Sixth Avenue and Battle Street in downtown Kamloops. It's a bright airy room with large windows giving a good view to the North. On Christmas Eve, when Kathy James placed her call, the Kamloops Telecoms Centre was colourfully decorated to celebrate the holiday season.

Communications operators are a critical and essential component in modern-day police work. For police officers in the field, particularly those in remote areas, the operators are literally their lifeline. RCMP communications operators undergo a rigorous security check prior to employment. They must be high-school graduates and able to type 60 words per minute. More importantly, RCMP communications operators bring a "take charge" attitude to the job. Consequently, they're sharp, alert and of necessity, absolutely precise about everything they do.

Once hired, new operators begin an on-the-job three-month training course using a dual-control patch-in headset to the radio/telephone console. Newly hired operators sit next to their trainer, listen to all calls and learn the fast-paced RCMP communications routine firsthand. They call the training program "the buddy system."

In the communications centre, nothing is left to chance; RCMP procedures are rigidly followed at all times and operators have to b as much in control of communications procedures as the officers they're assisting. Failure to follow RCMP protocol could have deadly consequences. During difficult situations, such as the one that was developing on the West Pavilion Road, Telecoms operators are as much on edge as the responding officers.

The communications centre provides operators with a multi-line telephone switchboard, plus radio contact to police cars and the outlying subdivision detachments. Communications operators have immediate access to the Criminal Name Index (CNI), the central computerized registry located in Ottawa, that records the name and relevant details of any person who has been fingerprinted during the course of a police investigation. A CNI query from a communications operator results in an immediate printout on the person in question if their name is in the index.

Motor vehicle records are also easily accessed by Telecoms operators and a print out of all relevant vehicle information on the driver and the car is immediately available to the police officer. The Criminal Name Index is an important function of the Canadian Police Information Centre (CPIC). RCMP regulations require a CPIC inquiry to be initiated at all times before stopping a vehicle. It's an absolutely critical step in the investigative process.

As the pursuit of Rusty Michell up the West Pavilion Road continued, pursuant to RCMP procedure, Corpo-

Kamloops Telecoms Centre.

ral Gary Mydlak, the Watch Commander for the shift, had taken up a position in the Telcoms centre. Mydlak was a stocky barrel-chested man with a great booming voice. In order to follow the radio conversation between Madeline Riley and Constable Stan Walstrom in PC Twenty-Two Alpha Three, Corporal Mydlak had pulled up a chair and plugged a telephone handset into the dual- control training patch on the communications console.

On the West Pavilion Road tension was mounting. RCMP Constable Stan Walstrom now had a solid visual confirmation on Rusty Michell. This was not a good situation. Michell was not stopping, nor did Walstrom think he would.

To break the tension, Stan Walstrom told Keith McKay about the first time he'd arrested Rusty Michell. "He's a tough son-of-a-bitch," he said to McKay. I remember I'd just been posted to Lillooet, I was green as hell and we got a call to Ross's Taxi stand. When we got there it was easy to see he'd really pounded one on his lady. She was leaning against the wall of the building, trying to hide, I took a good look at her, she was a hell of a mess and one eye was beginning to close. It took two of us to cuff Michell, and even cuffed he fought so goddam hard that when I tried to get him around to the backdoor of the car we both slipped and fell on our butts on the street."

Stan Walstrom continued, "But you know, later I got to know the guy when he was sober. Those times he wasn't a bad guy." Stan laughed, remembering an incident. "For a time, Michell had to do some weekends at our lockup. On a couple or three of those occasions I was working the Friday night shift and I booked him in. We'd talk, he was OK."

Stan paused, they were approaching a blind corner to the left, there was nothing ahead but the night air, indicating a straight drop to the Fraser River. Stan took the corner carefully, his headlights shining into the empty night, he got around the corner, saw Michell about ten car lengths ahead and stepped on the gas to close the distance between the two cars.

"Nice night for a quiet drive up a mountain," he said to Keith McKay "Anyway . . . so he'd come in for his mandatory weekends and we'd talk. Then, I'd see him on the street during the next week and I'd say. 'Hi, how's it going?' and he'd kinda ignore me."

Stan had an easy laugh, he carried on chuckling about Michell and said, "Geez, so one night he comes in for his weekend slammer time and says to me, Walstrom you shouldn't talk to me on the street. Some body might figure I like cops." Stan laughed again and said, "This guy has a real attitude problem, believe me."

Keith grinned, it was good to lighten up for the moment. But, they both knew they were in a serious situation and it was absolutely critical to stay right on top of Michell. They were well aware of his vicious side and knew from his criminal record and violent mood swings, that if provoked, he was easily capable of killing. The West Pavilion Road is heavily treed, and if Michell got out of their sight, left his car and managed to find cover in the darkened woods, the drunk, yet wily Michell could easily allude them.

Stan Walstrom carried on telling Keith about Michell, "You know why he's prohibited from carrying firearms?"

Keith didn't know.

"Well I remember seeing this when I was going over his files. It happened one night when there was a big party at his sister's house, Rusty got pissed off at something someone had said, went outside, got his gun out his car and fired the goddamn thing right through the open front door of the house."

"Sounds like a real neat guy to take to a party," Keith said dryly.

"Yeah, no kidding," Stan laughed at Keith's response, then continued on about the incident. "There were kids in the house and everything. Anyway, that little stunt got him a five-year prohib on carrying firearms."

The police car radio toned on, Kamloops operator Riley was calling back. "Alpha Three, Kamloops here. What speed are you doing now?"

"Fifty-nine kilometres, up the gravel road here."

"10-4."

At that point Watch Commander Mydlak checked in with PC Twenty-Two Alpha Three, his voice booming through the police car radio.

"Corporal Mydlak here."

Mydlak's transmission came in broken, but there was no mistaking the big familiar voice. Walstrom replied, "Go ahead, Gary."

Watch commanders keep their dialogue to a minimum, providing supervisory assistance only when necessary. Communications operator Madeline Riley responded: "He's just confirming that he is monitoring."

Walstrom confirmed the transmission, "10-4, recognize the voice there. We're doing 50 kilometres up the hill. Subject all over the road. He's spraying the vehicle, the police vehicle with rocks and stuff. Just passed the 17 kilometre mark doing 55 kilometres an hour."

The West Pavilion Road climbs in altitude as it proceeds north and as at did, there was more and more snow on the ground and on the road. When Walstrom and McKay left Lillooet that evening, the roads had been wet and bare with only patches of ice. Now, 17 kilometres into the West Pavilion hills along the narrow logging road, they were running into heavier snow and glare ice.

Rusty Michell's driving was becoming more and more erratic. At times he'd speed up, almost losing control of the big Olds and skidding to the edge of the road, then recovering and slowing down.

Stan Walstrom was getting nervous, his voice strained. "Kamloops, we're following about three vehicle lengths behind, travelling 49 kilometres an hour."

At that point the breaking communications signals combined with the RCMP paramilitary-style operations overuse of numerical jargon provided a bit of comic diversion. Kamloops Telecoms queried his broadcast, "49? 10 -4"

Walstrom, dead serious, now nervous as hell, forgetting his last transmission and thinking he'd been misunderstood earlier about the pursuit, responded. "Subject is reported to be 68 well, so that's the reason we're following."

The number 68, in the statute-law references used so often by police forces, indicates an impaired driver. Telecoms, understanding the confusion, left it alone and replied: "10-4."

At this point that Constables Walstrom and McKay began to worry about Rusty Michell's condition and more particularly his motives. With the piercing police-car takedown beams completely lighting up the interior of Michell's car, they could see him look down, and with absolutely no concern for his own safety, take both hands off the steering wheel and dig around on the car seat as if he'd misplaced something.

"Geez, look at that!" Stan Walstrom said to Keith McKay, "The stupid bugger just took both hands off the steering wheel. Shit, he's gonna go over the edge." But nothing happened, Michell looked up again at the road, took the steering wheel, straightened the car and kept driving up the West Pavilion Road.

Stan Walstrom called quickly called this information in, "Kamloops, he's reaching down into his right for some reason and we're slowed down to 32 kilometres an hour."

There was a critical reason why Michell was reaching down to the seat and before the night was over his actions would become tragically clear.

It was now three minutes past eight o'clock, Christmas Eve 1993, twenty-one minutes since Kathy James had run in panic across the Bridge River Indian Reserve road to her aunt's house and called for help. Just nine minutes since PC Twenty-Two Alpha Three spotted Rusty Michell and the Olds 88 speeding south on the Moha Road. For some the night would soon be over, for others it was just beginning.

Communications operator Riley didn't want the three-minute radio repeater timer to switch off and she advised Stan Walstrom she going to reset it. "10-4 Alpha Three. I'm just going to put the repeater down so you don't lose it."

Walstrom responded, "10-4."

Repeater locked on, Riley quickly called back to Walstrom. "OK Alpha Three, what's happening?"

"Oh, we're still following him about two and a half vehicle lengths and, uh, he's ignoring everything. He's, uh, obviously knows he's been followed. We're doing 55 kilometres an hour."

Michell had picked up speed, the green Olds weaving from side to side and he certainly knew he was being followed.

"You know this guy's been fighting the law for all of his life and tonight isn't going to be any different." Stan Walstrom said to Keith McKay.

"Yeah," Keith McKay replied, then added, "He wants some space, I guess."

Stan continued, "Even if he's falling down drunk, he's a big, tough bugger and if we physically have to get at it, you and I are going to have our hands full, believe me."

Keith stayed cool, he wasn't as excitable as Stan Walstrom. "We'll manage," he replied.

To both officers it was clear that Rusty Michell desperately wanted to put some distance between himself and the piercing RCMP take-down lights which represented the law and authority he found so oppressive. But McKay understood better than Walstrom, that Rusty Michell was probably running from a lot of things. As they climbed higher into the West Pavilion Hills, Keith thought, maybe Rusty was searching for a quiet place, a spiritual retreat, maybe he's trying to outrun his own anger.

There was no doubt that Michell had an intense hate for the white society and everything it represented. It mattered little that both police officers in pursuit of him were themselves status Indians, Michell didn't know, or care.

Back in Lillooet, Al Olsen left his house, got in his police car, identified as Twenty-Two Alpha Four, started the motor and called Stan Walstrom.

Olsen's commanding voice came over the police car radio: "Where you at Stan?"

"Twenty-one kilometres up West Pavilion, chasing Rusty Michell. Not really chasing him, we're just trying to get him to pull over."

Olsen knew Stan Walstrom had been working the Christmas Eve shift alone, so he queried Walstrom's use of the plural "we."

"You got somebody with you?"

The transmission between the two police cars was coming in broken. Walstrom hadn't heard the question.

"10-9?" He asked.

Olsen repeated his query. "You got someone with you?"

"I got Keith McKay, STNP, with me."

Walstrom's response was an immediate relief to Al Olsen. He knew STNP Constable Keith McKay as a good officer. He was experienced in police procedures and brought a calm, composed attitude to the job. Plus, it was

RCMP policy that assistance must be called in when an officer responded to a domestic violence call on an Indian reserve.

Before starting out on the West Pavilion Road, Al Olsen had to first stop off at the Main Street RCMP detachment and pick up his Smith and Wesson .38 Police Special revolver. He called back to Stan Walstrom:

"OK, I'm going to be along quickly. I've got to stop at the office for a second, and I'll be on my way."

In 1993, the RCMP began a change-over of police car colours. The royal blue paint scheme, in place for twenty years was replaced by a white paint exterior, with decals applied to mark the car with the appropriate RCMP insignia. RCMP research had found that white vehicles with contrasting reflective markings increase the car's visibility. That night, and since he was on call, Al Olsen had taken a police car home. It was a new car for the Lillooet detachment and the first car in Lillooet with the white paint job.

As Olsen quickly backed the new RCMP Chevrolet Police Standard Caprice out of his driveway, he found the toggle switches that activate the flashing emergency equipment and headed the two and half kilometres down the hillside residential streets of Lillooet to the RCMP detachment office.

During the drive downtown, Al Olsen could see his quiet Christmas Eve at home rapidly falling apart. It had started out so well. Following a long day at the office, Al had gone home, poured a drink for his wife Joan and himself, then the couple had made supper. After dinner they sat down to watch TV. Al's parents had phoned from Alberta wishing everyone a Merry Christmas. The bars would close at 8:00 that night and there was every reason to believe that this was going to be an uneventful night.

Al mused about the situation: "Shit, here I am at five minutes past eight on Christmas Eve, speeding past the Christmas tree lights on my street down to the police station to get my gun. I have two young police officers twenty kilometres out of town on a lonely and dangerous logging road, in hot pursuit of a wacked-out, probably armed, predictably-violent, wife-beating Indian." "Geez, peace on earth," he said to himself.

It had already been a tough day for Al Olsen. The previous evening, two young vandals had broken into nine parked cars on a residential Lillooet street. The boys had painted the cars with pressurized spray-paint cans and broken the windows to gain access. From a few of the cars they'd stolen presents that had been locked up for Christmas-day surprise safe keeping. The boys had later been apprehended, and Al Olsen had spent most of his Christmas Eve day shift processing the arrest details and ensuring the recovered presents were returned to their rightful owners.

Stan Walstrom was back on the police-band radio: "10-4. Al, he's reported to be 68 impaired and has gone and destroyed a little bit of the house there. So, that's why we're trying to get a hold of him."

Al Olsen responded: "10-4."

As Al Olsen drove down the hill to the RCMP detachment, Telecoms operator Madeline Riley had talked again with Kathy James and provided the first positive news of the night.

"Alpha Three, Kamloops, we've contacted the wife. She has the kids, the kids are not in the car. There are two weapons in the house, she's just going to go check to see if they're still there, or if he might have them."

For Stan Walstrom, that news was a major relief. He said to Keith McKay, "God, it's good to hear she's got all the kids. He could have made things pretty hairy for us if he had any of the kids in the car."

But the comment about Michell having a weapon was cause for concern. Stan Walstrom was sure Michell had a rifle on the front seat of his car. Walstrom relayed his concerns to Madeline Riley.

"10-4. He was reaching for something there earlier, as we remarked, so if you want to make sure that's indicated at the time."

Then, with the police car microphone off, Walstrom said to McKay, "But maybe he was just reaching for a beer, or a smoke."

McKay was skeptical and replied, "Yeah, could be, but whatever he's doing, it means at no time can we let him out of our sight. If he has a rifle and even if it's on the back seat, this guy is still dangerous."

In Lillooet, Al Olsen turned left off Main Street and drove into the RCMP detachment parking lot. He ran up to the door, unlocked it, went to his corner office, took his Sam Browne belt and holster out of the desk drawer, flipped open the cylinder on the Police Special .38 to check that the gun was fully loaded, then he put on the belt.

As Olsen left the detachment building, 23 kilometres behind Stan Walstrom, Communications Operator Madeline Riley was advising Walstrom that Rusty Michell was armed. "OK, the lady's just on line now, she cannot find the 30.30. The other gun is there, she cannot find the 30.30." As Stan Walstrom would learn later, Kathy James gave the wrong description, that night Rusty Michell had his Lee Enfield .303.

Al Olsen had to be sure Stan Walstrom had heard about the rifle. "You copy, Stan?"

Walstrom responded, his voice nervous, he was repeating himself, the pressure was mounting.

"Copy that, Kamloops, thank you. Twenty-Two Alpha Three, copy that. We're travelling 42 kilometres an hour . . . and we're about two vehicle lengths behind the guy, all our lights are activated, wig- wags, dome, dome lights are on as well."

To add to the tension, at kilometre 24 the road conditions were rapidly deteriorating. Walstrom advised Kamloops. "The road is really slippery and has compact snow with gravel and gravel covered ice."

Watch Commander Corporal Mydlak needed to know how well Stan Walstrom was armed. "Twenty-Two Alpha Four. Do you have a shotgun in that vehicle?"

Walstrom responded in the affirmative. "10-4."

In fact, all rural detachment police cars carry a Remington 12- gauge shotgun which is cradled in a steel mount on the transmission hump between the front seats of the car. The gun is loaded, but it is against regulations to have a shell in the chamber, while the gun is in the car. Hovey Industries of Mississauga, Ontario makes the mount.

For safety purposes, the end of the shotgun barrel sits in a heavy steel well. If the gun was ever accidentally discharged while in the mount, the large-diameter SSG pellets would be contained in the well. The shotgun is secured in the mount by a steel clasp that fits over the barrel at mid-length. The clasp is locked with an electronically controlled locking mechanism. To unlock the clasp and remove the shotgun, the police car motor must be running. Then, there is normally a spring-loaded toggle switch, mounted in a panel on the dashboard. The toggle is held on with one hand, leaving the other hand to open the clasp and remove the shotgun. In a situation where speedy removal of the shotgun is required, the police officer can hold the toggle switch open with one hand, grab the pistol grip of the shotgun with the other and lift straight up, using the shotgun barrel to open the locking clasp. Twenty-Two Alpha Four had a different shotgun unlocking mechanism as Al Olsen would learn later that evening.

Watch Commander Mydlak needed to check out Constable Keith McKay's status as a police officer.

"And is it an Auxiliary that you have with you?"

"He's a member of the Tribal Police," Walstrom responded.

The British Columbia Police Act has a section that deals with the appointment of special constables. The act is designed specifically for aboriginal police officers and gives the appointed special constable the powers, duties and immunities of a provincial constable, in other words, the same status as a police officer in any of the province's municipal police forces.

Sergeant Al Olsen needed to know if Keith McKay had his provincial appointment: "Keith, you said you had your appointment now didn't you?"

Stan Walstrom answered: "10-4, he has his appointment."

This was a crucial answer. Without an appointment McKay could not carry a gun or fire a weapon if called upon to do so. With McKay's appointment confirmed, Al Olsen asked about the weapons the two officers were carrying: "Both you and this other member are armed?"

"10-4."

That information was critical to Al and meant that both officers had their .38 Police Special revolvers plus the Remington 12 gauge shotgun. By now, Olsen was well on his way out of Lillooet; he had crossed the Bridge River bridge and was on the West Pavilion logging road. Because he hadn't yet reached the glare-ice conditions of the higher elevations, he was pounding the Chevy Caprice along the narrow gravel track as fast as he could. On the straight stretches between the switchbacks and blind corners, he was reaching speeds in excess of 110 kilometres an hour.

It was a nerve-wracking pursuit. Al Olsen didn't know the road; there were no guard rails, no warning signs, just steep hills on the right and for much of the road a sheer drop to the Fraser River on the left, but he did know he had to catch up with PC Twenty-Two Alpha Three, and Rusty Michell as quickly as possible. Police officers are trained that the longer they are in control of any situation involving a suspect, the more likely it is that they will arrest or contain the suspect.

It was absolutely essential that Walstrom and McKay maintain visual contact with Rusty Michell and, given that the suspect was armed, it was important for Al Olsen to provide backup at the arrest scene when, and if, it happened. He knew now that Michell had a rifle somewhere in the car, and like most avid hunters, was no doubt an excellent shot. Plus, and it was a big plus, Michell wasn't bound by RCMP deadly-force regulations that required the shooter to warn, draw, point and then fire. Michell also had a 200 metre shooting advantage. The Police Special .38 revolvers had limited range and the police-issue 12 gauge shotguns, even with their tight-pattern SSG shot would not be effective at all in a rifle shoot-out with Rusty

Michell. If the situation turned nasty, Walstrom and McKay needed all the manpower assistance they could get.

Stan Walstrom called in again confirming his position and the worsening road conditions: "Kamloops, just passing the 26 kilometre mark, we're doing 32 kilometres an hour, really icy here with gravel and gravel-covered ice."

Al Olsen needed to know if he was gaining on the pursuit, and he used a reference on Highway 99, on the east side of the Fraser River, to pose his question. "Where does that put you, Stan, out past Houghton on the other side?"

Walstrom responded with a similar reference to Highway 99: "Actually, we're quite a ways past that, we're out past the 12-mile area. We're actually closer to Pavilion."

Stan Walstrom paused, then had a nagging thought about Madeline Riley's previous comment that Michell had two rifles at home. He called this request in: "Kamloops can you confirm with the original complainant and have her check and see if she knows where the weapons were? Or if any other family members have them?" Stan Walstrom knew Michell had at least one rifle with him, but if this pursuit was going to end up in a shoot out, it was essential to know what other weapons Michell might be carrying.

In the brightly-lit Kamloops communication centre, Watch Commander Gary Mydlak asked Telecoms operator Riley for more information about the weapons Michell may have with him. "You still talking to that lady? Stan wants to make sure no other family members have his rifle. When did she last see it there? Is there a possibility someone else may have had the rifle?"

Madeline Riley called Kathy James back, if the rifle was missing, but in the hands of anyone other than Rusty

Michell, Walstrom and McKay were in a far better position.

Back on the West Pavilion logging road, Michell's behavior and driving were becoming more and more erratic. The big Oldsmobile was running poorly. At times it would speed up, the rear tires spinning out and sliding the car sideways. Then it would slow down, as if it had engine problems.

A few minutes later, a nervous Stan Walstrom called in again:

"Kamloops, Alpha Three. Obviously . . . uh, just to let you know we're coming up to the 28, the 28 kilometre mark and the subject has rolled his window down. We're following him at 37 kilometres an hour. He's rolled his window down."

That comment caused immediate concern for Al Olsen. This was not a good situation. The green Oldsmobile had power windows and were easy to lower. Either Rusty Michell in his intoxicated state simply needed some fresh air, or he was planning something. Olsen was thinking the worst, if Michell, when he was seen reaching down to his right, had his rifle next to him in the front seat, was he considering firing a shot at the pursuing police car?

Then there was the distinct possibility that he had another person with him. After all, he had been partying with a number of friends, maybe one of them, unnoticed by Kathy James, had come along for the ride.

Since Olsen didn't have the advantage of seeing what Stan could of the Oldsmobile's interior, he called Walstrom to raise this concern. "Stan, is there more than one person in that vehicle?"

"Not that we can see."

As the officer in charge, Al Olsen's concern for Walstrom and McKay was growing as the pursuit continued. From his twenty years of experience he knew nothing could be left to chance. From what Olsen had heard about Michell's record, he was, if anything, totally unpredictable.

"You watch, and make sure he doesn't get a gun out there at you."

Stan Walstrom replied, "10-4."

Al Olsen's high speeds and aggressive pursuit along the narrow side-hill road were beginning to pay off. He called in his up-dated position to Stan Walstrom: "I just passed the 15-kilometre mark." Olsen had started out 23 kilometres behind Stan Walstrom and was now only 13 kilometres back and gaining.

Kamloops communications called in. Madeline Riley had spoken again to Kathy James and could now confirm that Michell had only one rifle with him, and that no one else but Rusty could have taken it that evening.

"Alpha Three, Kamloops, she says he definitely has the rifle. It was there, she says, and now it's not, so he definitely has it."

5

THE WEST PAVILION LOGGING ROAD runs in a northerly direction along the Fraser River and ends 100 kilometres from Lillooet at the Big Bar Creek ferry. This is a water-reaction ferry crossing the Fraser River at the point where Big Bar Creek enters the river. Water-reaction ferries are used commonly in remote areas in British Columbia but, because of their design, operate only when the river is open and free from ice. During the winter season, when ice is on the river, an elevated cable car replaces the ferry.

A water-reaction ferry is connected to cables strung across the river. The ferry, essentially a deck on pontoons, is attached to the cross cables by a right-side and left-side set of cables, with the bow pointing upstream. By adjusting the lengths of the cables, the operator angles the bow of the ferry at an angle into the current and the force of the river current moves the ferry across the river. It's the same reaction concept as a sailboat sailing into the wind. A water-reaction ferry is not complicated and requires only one operator. It is cheaper than a bridge, though certainly not as seasonally practical.

Neither Stan Walstrom, Keith McKay nor Al Olsen had been as far up the West Pavilion Road as the Big Bar ferry. Walstrom wondered if the ferry was operating. If it was, and Rusty Michell kept going he could conceivably cross the Fraser River and continue on to the Highway 97 community of Clinton.

Stan Walstrom asked Al Olsen if the RCMP Clinton Detachment should be called on for assistance. "Do we want to contact Clinton now and have them come up on the other side?"

Al Olsen had his doubts about that suggestion. With the Fraser River between them, counting on backup from the Clinton Detachment was a marginal suggestion at best. He also thought it wasn't too likely that the Big Bar Creek crossing was operational at this time of the year. And even on the remote chance it was running, there sure as hell wouldn't be an operator waiting around for his little parade at nine o'clock at night on Christmas Eve.

He replied to Walstrom: "I don't know whether you can get across on the ferry, I doubt if it's running."

At that point the RCMP officer on duty at Clinton broke in. "Yeah Lillooet, this is Clinton Detachment, where are you?"

Stan Walstrom replied, but he knew there was little chance of help from the neighboring detachment:

"We're heading up towards Big Bar Creek, I'm unfamiliar with the area. OK, we're on a service road, called West Pavilion Road, we're headed northbound, uh . . . basically heading towards Clinton, an area called Big Bar . . . still following the subject here."

The Clinton officer replied: "You said you're about 21 kilometres, is that 21 K from Lillooet? I'm looking at a not very reliable map here."

Stan Walstrom could tell this conversation was going nowhere. "We're actually 29 kilometres out on West Pavilion Road, which is north of Lillooet, which actually has us travelling northwest on West Pavilion Road. We just passed the 29 kilometre mark and we're doing 38 kilometres an hour."

Clinton RCMP needed more information in order to locate the pursuit route on a map. "The West Pavilion Road you're on now, it branched off the Moha Road?"

Walstrom replied, "10-4. That's correct."

The response from the Clinton Detachment was not at all encouraging. "I think I've got a map where you're at. I don't think I can get out there to give you a hand at blocking your suspect off. This time of the year, there's no hope of us getting across the Fraser and getting anywhere near you."

This was the response Stan Walstrom thought he'd hear. He and McKay were clearly all alone in this pursuit. Their only backup was Al Olsen still some ten kilometres back, and, on these roads probably fifteen minutes behind. A lot could go wrong in fifteen minutes. Walstrom acknowledged the Clinton communication and continued with an update: "Copy that, we're still about three vehicle lengths behind him, doing 26 kilometres an hour, keeping an eye out on the open window."

Two kilometres farther down the ice-covered road, Stan Walstrom thought they may get their first break, Michell's car was acting up again.

"Kamloops, we're just passing the 31-kilometre mark, sounds like he's having engine problems. Possibly running out of gas, is what it sounds like, he's choking and sputtering here a bit and we're on a downhill grade and he's coasting and we're doing 30 kilometres an hour."

Stan Walstrom was sounding nervous, he repeated his comment about Michell's car and informed Kamloops Telecoms Centre that he and Keith McKay were ready to shoot Michell, if deadly force was required."

The vehicle still choking and sputtering here. We're taking it rather seriously, we have our sidearms ready, mine's unsnapped and prepared. His engine's really acting up and he's gonna run out of gas here shortly."

Anticipating that Walstrom and McKay were soon to be involved in a serious confrontation, Watch Commandeer Gary Mydlak needed to know where Al Olsen was in relation to the younger officers. "How far behind are you, Alpha Four?"

Stan Walstrom, nervously preoccupied with the quickly unfolding events, thought Kamloops was requesting his position instead of Olsen's in Alpha Four. His response underscored the tension he was experiencing. "We're about four vehicle lengths behind right now, maybe five."

Al Olsen didn't like the way the situation was developing. Clearly, Walstrom was on edge. If Michell's engine stalled or his car ran out of gas, it was certain to trigger a violent reaction in the native man.

They knew Rusty was armed, and after thirty minutes of having a police car on his tail with all its emergency lights flashing, it was pretty obvious he had no intention of surrendering peacefully. On top of this, Olsen was now running into the higher-elevation ice on the West Pavilion Road. He had to start taking it easy; there was no way he could provide backup if his car went off the road. Olsen relayed his concerns to Stan Walstrom. "Just passing the 21-kilometre mark. I'm going to be slower now Stan, because I'm starting to run into your ice."

Walstrom could hear Olsen's concern coming through the police car radio transmission. "10-4. We just passed the 32 kilometre mark. We're using extreme caution, making sure not to get too close."

Al Olsen's next transmission came through loud and clear. Stan Walstrom could hear and almost feel the intense determination in Olsen's voice. This was no longer a conversation between two policemen. A direct order was being given to a subordinate by a seasoned police officer. A commanding officer with twenty years experience who had faced this type of unpredictable danger before. "Stan, if he exits the vehicle with a rifle and gets in the dark . . . you get the hell out of there."

Stan Walstrom had no problem with that advice. "10-4", he replied.

Michell's driving continued to be erratic; he'd slow down, then speed up. When his vehicle was slowed, he kept reaching down toward his right. Stan Walstrom was convinced Michell had his rifle in the front seat.

Walstrom called in, "Kamloops, we're travelling about six vehicle lengths behind him."

"10-4. What kind of speed now?"

Michell had quickened the pace. "We're doing 53 kilometres and I'm passing the 33 kilometre mark."

Al Olsen wanted to reconfirm that there were no children involved. "Stan what's the status on the kids again, 10-9?"

"Complainant said he dropped them, said he just dropped them off." Then he added, "I don't think he ever had them."

"OK, so we know there's no kids in the vehicle."

"10-4."

Stan Walstrom next asked Al Olsen on the advisability of stopping the pursuit and putting a roadblock in place.

"Twenty-Two Alpha Three, Al . . . what about a road block?"

Al Olsen did not like this suggestion at all. "Not a good move. If this guy gets out in the dark with a loaded rifle and we're standing around at a road block, we're in big trouble. We've confirmed with the wife that the suspect has a gun. . . We suspect he has it in the front seat . . . We know there's no kids to worry about. . . We maintain control and keep the suspect in sight. No way can we allow this guy to get out of view. If he's in the dark and we're in the open, we're big easy targets, we've got bull's eyes painted all over us. Stay on his tail, stay with the suspect."

"10-4."

Stan Walstrom brought the police cruiser closer to Rusty Michell's green Oldsmobile. He had more information for Al Olsen.

"We had a visual with him here, also, Al. We've been close enough to have a look. We can see a red light on his . . . in the cab of his vehicle, I don't know if it's a seat-belt light, or an engine light, or something, but he's still having problems with his engine."

Al Olsen thought, the alert is on. If Michell's motor failed, the confrontation with the angry young native would happen quickly. Would Michell surrender quietly, or would he use his rifle in an attempt to shoot his way free? He asked for an update on Stan Walstrom's position.

"What's your 20 now, Stan?" But the radio transmission came in broken. Stan Walstrom hadn't heard the question.

"Again?"

"What's your 20?"

This time the signal was clearer. Walstrom called in, his voice anxious, he expected something to happen soon. Rusty Michell's driving was becoming more and more erratic. With the temperature dropping the road conditions were deteriorating badly and the motor in the green Oldsmobile was continuing to act up.

"We should be approaching the 35-kilometre mark, we're on heavy . . . heavy compact snow and glare ice with some gravel on it. He's all over the road and it appears that he's having problems with his engine again. We're just coming up to a kilometre sign now. It's the 36- kilometre coming up. Copy that? 36."

Kamloops asked Walstrom about his speed. "10-4. And the speed?"

"48 kilometres an hour."

Al Olsen, still 10 kilometres behind, called in his position. "Twenty-Two Alpha Four is at 26."

Al Olsen was worried. Stan Walstrom's last message had given him a lot of reasons to be seriously concerned. If the green Oldsmobile stalled, a shoot-out with Rusty Michell was imminent. Michell was keeping his speed up to 50 kilometres an hour, and although Al Olsen was travelling considerably faster, he was not catching up to PC Twenty- Two Alpha Three as quickly as he would have liked to.

Al Olsen relayed his fears to Stan Walstrom. "I'm probably not going to be able to catch up to you, Stan, because I probably can't do much better in terms of speed than you can."

Walstrom understood, but that didn't help. The roads were getting considerably more dangerous, Rusty Michell was skidding from side to side, yet every time Walstrom thought the big Olds was going to hit the ditch, Michell would recover and manage to get the car back on the narrow icy logging road. Then there was the question of the rifle. Where was it? In the front seat, or the back seat, or was it in the trunk? Not too likely it's in the trunk, Walstrom thought. Sure as hell, there were going to be shots fired before this night was over. He needed help, advice, anything to help him at least be mentally prepared for the unknown.

"10-4, Al. I know how it is. . . Uh, what do you suggest from here, because I don't want to be dealing with this guy with a rifle." A critical element of police training is knowing how to maintain a safe physical distance in any potentially dangerous situation. A sober trouble maker is approached far differently than a falling-down drunk. The RCMP teach recruits that a man with a knife is considered dangerous at a distance of six metres. A man with a rifle is a deadly threat at 200 metres. In the wooded West Pavilion area, Rusty Michell had a tremendous advantage, both in terms of cover and firepower, over Stan Walstrom and Keith McKay.

Al Olsen racked his brain thinking of the best way to describe safe-distance strategy and common sense tactics to an obviously nervous Stan Walstrom. His sentence structure was slightly fractured but the message was brutally direct.

"Well . . . Stan, make sure you give yourself a cushion with the vehicle to start with, that's the biggest thing. If he steps out there with a gun and takes off, you gotta be prepared to get out of there. In the dark, we're not going in there after him, we get outta there, 'til we know where he is. If he steps out with out the gun, well . . . then, the two of you should be able to deal with him."

Walstrom replied, "10-4. Copy that, hopefully he doesn't get out with the gun."

Al Olsen needed to check out the firepower situation in PC Twenty Two Alpha Three. "Stan, is Keith qualified for a shotgun?"

"10-4."

"Do you have it out, Keith?"

Stan Walstrom answered. "Negative. We're just passing the 37 kilometre mark, we're doing 49 kilometres an hour, downhill, we're about to take the shotgun out of the mount."

A 12-gauge shotgun will do tremendous damage at short range and an accidental discharge in the car would be devastating. An unintended shot could blow a hole through the floor of the car. Al Olsen didn't want any unplanned surprises.

He warned Keith McKay about trying to pump-action a shell into the shotgun's chamber while driving. "Don't chamber a round in the vehicle, OK, please?"

Walstrom got the point and appreciated the genuine concern Olsen had for the younger policemen's safety. "10-4. Copy. We're sure he has a shotgun or his rifle actually. Al, Michell is doing 28 kilometres an hour and we're about six lengths behind him. All our lights are still activated."

Michell had slowed down again. Olsen felt somewhat encouraged. "That's good. If you can stay at that speed, I'm gonna catch up to you."

Rusty Michell continued to just maintain control of the Oldsmobile on the ice-covered mountain road. But he was still clearly preoccupied with whatever was on the car seat down to his right.

"Kamloops, he's trying to grab something his right, I can't see exactly what it is. However, he's . . . he's reach-

ing down for something there. We're passing the 38 kilometre mark and approaching a curve, a sharp curve." Then
Stan Walstrom's voice became more excited. Michell was
heading into the corner, seemingly out of control.

"Geez, Michell just about went into the ditch, there."
But, amazingly, Rusty Michell wrestled the big Oldsmobile
back onto the road.

It was now 8:30, Christmas Eve. Forty eight minutes
had passed since Kathy James had first called the RCMP
for help. What had started out as a domestic dispute at
the Bridge River Indian Reserve was now a full-fledged
code-three pursuit.

Rusty Michell had attracted not only the attention of
the RCMP, but some of his friends as well. Wayne Redan,
an acquaintance of Kathy James and Rusty Michell, had
a police radio scanner. He'd tuned in the police frequency
and was following the Michell pursuit with some interest. It wasn't often that a police car chase or anything he'd
ever heard on the scanner, lasted so long or with such in-
tensity. Stan Walstrom had used Rusty Michell's name a
number of times on the car radio, and Wayne knew exactly who the police were talking about.

Wayne was having a Christmas party that evening and
had a whole crowd of people at his house. The police radio scanner would become the focus of their attention for
the evening. Wayne called Kathy, told her about the chase
and how far Rusty had led the police out of town.

Kathy's fear for her own safety quickly changed to a
larger concern for Rusty. He had a terrible temper. She
knew he had one of his rifles and she hadn't seen him so
violent in some time. In fact, until this evening, Rusty
hadn't been abusive to Kathy in well over two years. She

had no idea what had triggered his behavior, but tonight he'd been terrifying.

She began to regret calling the police. Russell Michell was a profoundly troubled man, but in spite of all his problems and his abusive nature, Kathy James loved him. He was the father of four of her five children. When sober, Rusty Michell was an attentive father and a good husband. He often took Kathy's oldest boy Kevin out hunting and encouraged all the children to do well at school. In happier times, Rusty liked to party and play music, he jammed a bit on the guitar and on occasion would play music with a group of friends from the Fountain Indian Reserve.

But tonight was not a happy time. Rusty was ripped and seething with anger. The pursuit continued. For a few minutes the police car radio was quiet, then Kamloops Telecoms requested an update. "Alpha Three, where you at?"

"We should be approaching the 41-kilometre mark here and cranked up to 65-kilometres an hour. We're still on compact snow and gravel covered and we're about eight vehicle lengths behind him. Just passing the 41-kilometre mark at a speed of 62 kilometres an hour."

6

TWENTY-TWO ALPHA FOUR, the police car Al Olsen was driving, had only recently arrived in Lillooet. In fact, tonight was the first he had driven the 1993 Chevrolet Caprice with its new-look white RCMP color scheme. He looked for the dash-mounted toggle switch unit that activates the shotgun release. Since there is no standard order for the five switches which control the emergency equipment and the shotgun mechanism, the switches have labels identifying their function. But the toggle switches on PC Twenty-Two Alpha Four had yet to be labeled. Because both hands have to be off the steering wheel to release the gun lock, Al Olsen needed to know where the shotgun toggle was located. On this terribly treacherous road and at the speed he was driving, he was not going try a no-hands-on-the-wheel experiment to find the shotgun switch.

Al Olsen called Stan Walstrom: "Stan, have you driven Alpha Four?"

"10-4. Copy. Yeah, I have, what's the problem?"

"Where's the shotgun toggle?"

"It's not a toggle, it's a button underneath the box on the far right."

"10-4. Thanks."

At the same time, Al Olsen thought if this situation starts to fall apart, if the shotgun release is wrong, I'd better be prepared for the worst. He unsnapped his Police .38 Special revolver, took it out of the holster and put it beside him on the passenger's seat of the police car. It was a move he'd never forget.

Back at the RCMP Telecoms Centre, Watch Commander Corporal Gary Mydlak was following the pursuit on the West Pavilion Road with a growing sense of unease and frustration. As watch commander for the Christmas Eve shift, he was technically in command, but in reality he was just another person listening to an unfolding set of events that might as well have been happening on the moon.

There was no further backup that could be provided. No way to put other RCMP officers in place for an intercept of Rusty Michell. All Gary Mydlak could do was listen to the pursuit on the Telecoms console, follow the kilometre markings on the map and try to be as helpful as he could. Mydlak called Stan Walstrom again, his voice booming out of the police car radio.

"Alpha Three. Watch commander. Be advised my map indicates your road is going to be deteriorating conditions further up and I read you at about Slok Creek."

Getting advice from someone sitting in a radio room in downtown Kamloops when he running into obviously perilous conditions 40 kilometres along an icy logging road was the last thing Stan Walstrom needed, but the young officer realized Gary Mydlak was simply doing all he could to help.

Walstrom responded, "10-4. It's wonderful out there Gary, thank you. We're just passing the 42 kilometre mark and we're doing 49 kilometres an hour."

A minute later Stan Walstrom gave Gary Mydlak another update. "He's about eight to ten vehicle lengths ahead of us and we still have our emergency lights activated. We're just passing the 43-kilometre mark and we're doing 61 kilometres an hour."

Al Olsen came on the radio giving his position. It wasn't good news, he hadn't closed the gap between his car and Stan Walstrom's as much as he'd hoped to.

"Kamloops. Twenty-Two Alpha Four. I'm at the 34-kilometre mark."

Telecoms operator Riley queried Al Olsen's position. "10-4. You only gained one kilometre all that way?"

"10-4. You got it. The road isn't all that good."

Stan Walstrom broke in to make Al Olsen's point. It was obvious he was concentrating on the icy road and not on the conversation. "Kamloops, the roads are really icy here. . . . Compact snow, gravel covered and we're going up a hill here. We're about ten vehicle-lengths with uh, . . . behind, with the vehicle in sight."

The West Pavilion Road was carved out of the steep side hills for industrial use and not for speed or ease of driving. For most of its length it clings precariously to the edge of the hills, continually twisting back on itself. Blind, sharp corners are common. A couple of times that night, the tight corners had caused Stan Walstrom to lose sight of Rusty Michell and the Oldsmobile. Walstrom couldn't allow that to happen again. He had arrested Rusty Michell too many times and knew he had enough aggressive hostility to take advantage of any delay in Walstrom's pursuit. If Michell figured he had enough distance between himself and the police car, he was certainly capable of stopping his car, quickly finding cover and opening fire with his rifle.

Stan Walstrom stepped on the gas, moving the Chevrolet Caprice closer to the Oldsmobile. The bright take-down lights lit up the interior of the Oldsmobile. Now, finally, Stan Walstrom could see what Rusty Michell had on his right.

"Shit, look at that," he said to Keith McKay. "He's got the fucking rifle sitting up on the seat right beside him. Geez, that's what he's been screwing around with when he's had his hands off the wheel. He's been trying to load the fucking gun." Stan Walstrom paused for a moment, then said, "Holy shit, that's the last thing we need"

Keith McKay, a bit more reserved than Stan Walstrom, replied, "Yeah, we're dealing with big fire power here." Then even more thoughtfully he said, "This situation can blow up in our face, or we can keep it under control. But whatever happens, we have to stick together and stay smart. If this guy thinks we're getting panicked, he'll be all over us like crap on a blanket."

Stan Walstrom nodded his head, they were now in a series of sharp corners. He had both hands on the wheel, concentrating totally on his driving. At this point the road straightened slightly, climbed in altitude and leveled out. Stan Walstrom backed off, putting a bit more distance between himself and Michell. Walstrom was now able to pick up the hand-held police car microphone and advise Kamloops of a positive identification on the rifle "Kamloops. Alpha Three. The rifle is sitting upright, Kamloops, copy that?"

Walstrom's nervousness was readily apparent, even over the static-scrambled radio transmission. He repeated himself. "The rifle is sitting upright, to his right, in between him and the passenger seat. We're now about 12 vehicle-lengths behind him."

In an attempt to learn if Al Olsen was closing the gap, Kamloops asked about Walstrom's speed.

"10-4. And Alpha Four, what kind of speed now, same?"

"We're doing 34 kilometres an hour and we just passed the 48. Extreme winter conditions . . . road conditions up here, with fog and minimal gravel, mostly compact snow."

The road and fog conditions were affecting Rusty Michell's driving too. Suddenly he went into a slide, the big Olds was moving sideways. Stan Walstrom shouted into the microphone: "He just hit the bank! He just went into the ditch! He's just losing control of his vehicle!"

Still many kilometres behind, Al Olsen thought, "This is it, he's stopped, it's show time."

But it wasn't to be, despite the ravages of a two-day drunk, Rusty Michell managed to recover. Stan Walstrom couldn't believe what he'd seen. "He got it back. He's still on the go. We're doing 20 kilometres an hour."

Meanwhile, Al Olsen was taking advantage of Michell's erratic driving speeds and the straight stretches, he was catching up to Stan Walstrom.

Kamloops then asked for an update on Olsen's progress and where he was in relation to Stan Walstrom. "Alpha Four, what's your twenty?"

Olsen responded, "I just passed 43."

That was encouraging and at the same time quite remarkable. Al Olsen was now only five kilometres behind Stan Walstrom. The time was 8:45, Christmas Eve. Olsen in PC Twenty-Two Alpha Four had left Lillooet at 8:09, 23 kilometres behind Walstrom. Now 36 minutes later, and under extremely hazardous mountain driving conditions, he was quickly closing the gap. With Stan Walstrom's visual confirmation of the rifle, plus the suspicion that Michell had somehow been able to load the rifle, while driving on this treacherous road, it would be in everyone's best interests if Al Olsen was on the scene when Michell was finally apprehended.

Just past the 48-kilometre mark, the West Pavilion Road forks. Rusty Michell took the fork to the right, which was the more travelled road. Stan Walstrom became concerned that Al Olsen might take the wrong road.

"Al, make sure you take the down road, when we, uh . . . when you come to it. Take the down road, not the up road."

Al Olsen needed more specific directions: "OK Stan. Whereabouts, where are you now, you mean take the down road around 48?"

"Yeah, 10-4. It's about a kilometre or so, or half a kilometre past the 48."

"OK. To the right, head down."

Rusty Michell was continuing to experience motor problems. His car would speed up, then slow down. Michell had turned on the Oldsmobile's interior lights, and Walstrom could see that Michell was still trying to load his rifle.

Walstrom called in. "Kamloops. His interior light is on. We're at the 49 kilometre mark and we're travelling 14 kilometres an hour. He's slowing down. . . like he's trying to bring us into him, but we're keeping our distance."

The strange parade continued. Michell in the green Oldsmobile. Stan Walstrom and Keith McKay in PC Twenty-Two Alpha Three. Five kilometres back, Al Olsen was quickly cutting down the distance between the two police cars. He drove past the 45-kilometre marker. In the next 30 minutes, the pursuit of Rusty Michell would be over.

7

THE SMITH AND WESSON MODEL 10 .38 Police Special has been the RCMP general-issue sidearm for the past forty years. It's a reliable revolver, and misfires are extremely rare. It has a five-inch barrel, holds six rounds, needs little maintenance and is reasonably inexpensive.

RCMP Smith and Wesson revolvers are loaded with a Federal Cartridge Company 158 grain hollow point bullet, which has a muzzle velocity of 890 feet per second. The cartridges are marked Federal .38 SPL + P. Most municipal police forces in Canada have switched to 9-millimetre automatic pistols, and the RCMP is planning a conversion to automatics in the future. An automatic pistol holds more rounds, reloads quickly and for these reasons is a superior weapon for police duty.

The British-built Lee Enfield Sussex .303 caliber rifle that Rusty Michell was carrying could be purchased in 1975 through the Eaton's catalogue for $57.00. It had a 5-shot magazine, a muzzle velocity of 2460 feet per second, a 22-inch barrel and a flat trajectory at 100 meters.

On Christmas Eve 1993, Al Olsen, Stan Walstrom and Keith McKay were carrying .38 Police Specials. Not the most effective weapons if they became engaged in a long-range shoot-out with Rusty Michell.

As the West Pavilion Road increased in altitude, the road conditions continued to deteriorate. Stan Walstrom called in: "Kamloops. We're now just hitting the 50- kilometre marker, doing 36 kilometres an hour. Extremely icy winter conditions. No gravel noted on the road. Suspect . . . he's slowing down considerably. Looks like he's having engine problems again." But Rusty Michell kept the Olds moving, sliding from side to side on the narrow road, the back end fishtailing on the compacted snow and ice.

At 8:51, one hour and nine minutes following Kathy James's call to the RCMP, Michell and Walstrom passed the 52-kilometre post. Walstrom called in his position.

Al Olsen responded. "I just passed 49." He was rapidly closing the distance between himself and Stan Walstrom. There was another fork in the road shortly after the 52 kilometre marking. One road goes to the left and up the hill. The other goes down towards the Fraser River to the right. Stan Walstrom was quick to pass on the directions to Al Olsen.

"As we speak we're just taking the Big Bar lower road, Al. So stay to the right, stay low, don't take the up road, stay right, copy?"

"10-4."

Following Walstrom's progress on his map, Watch Commander Corporal Gary Mydlak thought the pursuit was soon going to end as it seemed to him that they were approaching the Big Bar ferry. Although Olsen outranked Mydlak, regulations required that watch commander Mydlak have Sergeant Al Olsen, who was the senior officer in the pursuit, brief Stan Walstrom and Keith McKay. "Alpha Three, Watch Commander here, review procedures with your sergeant. What he wants done in the eventuality suspect stops with gun in hand, stops, stays in car and if you should receive hostile fire."

Al Olsen was quick to answer, his voice strong and determined. It was the same rigid set of orders he'd given that cold dark morning two years and ten months earlier on the Pinchie Reserve. A repeat of the instructions on the use of deadly force to Walstrom and McKay. "Stan if he comes out with a weapon, do like I say, get out of there, if he's gonna take a shot at you. If he goes in the dark, we can't chase in the dark. If he stays in the vehicle, just stay back, don't get out. If you can put the vehicle in position, protect yourself and use it, that's fine."

Al Olsen paused for a moment, his mike still open. Stan Walstrom and Keith McKay knew there was more to come. It did: "You and Keith are number one, your safety is first. If he returns fire at any time . . . take him out."

At this point the West Pavilion Road leaves a plateau high above the Fraser River and begins a twisty, but slow descent to the valley floor. Walstrom reported on the changing conditions: "We just passed the 53 kilometre mark, doing 32 kilometres an hour. Extremely poor road conditions, there's no fog now, our visibility is good. We're heading down a series of sharp turns . . . downhill . . . with a fairly substantial bank to our right."

Gary Mydlak was still convinced that the pursuit would soon end at the Big Bar Ferry and briefed Stan Walstrom again on Michell's record and RCMP apprehension procedures. "Alpha Three. Be advised the suspect is charged or convicted, 1988 careless use of firearms. Further on, be advised you can anticipate within the next few kilometres, the vehicle is not anticipated to pass the Big Bar ferry. If the suspect stays in the car, you order him out with a P.A., you order him to open the door with his left hand and keep his hands in full view and everything else is common sense. Good luck."

The advice from Gary Mydlak meant little to Stan Walstrom. He was the one who was going to be staring down Michell's rifle barrel when they stopped him, but Walstrom knew Watch Commander Mydlak was only trying to do his job.

"10-4. Copy that. Al, you have any other comments?"

"No, like I say, you gotta use your head here, and you gotta make sure that you take it easy." Olsen paused, trying his damnedest to give the men the best advice he could muster. "Don't get rushed or anything, your safety is first. Just remember, he's got that gun with him, he's been fooling around with it, he's got a past record of weapon assaults, so there's a good chance he's prepared to use it."

Within minutes Al Olsen would catch up to Stan Walstrom. Walstrom called out his position: "OK, we're just going by the 54-kilometre mark, two roads, stay low again, don't go up."

Olsen's reply was the best news Stan Walstrom had heard all evening. "10-4. I'm just about to the 53, so I'm not much over a kilometre behind you."

"10-4. Do you want to pass me Al, or what?"

"No, I'll follow you, Stan, and we'll hopefully get to the end down here. We'll get stopped and we'll make our play."

Gary Mydlak was still confused about the length of the West Pavilion Road and the distance to the Fraser River. The logging road kilometre markings were not on any of his maps and meant nothing. Gary Mydlak wanted to pin down their position and he queried Al Olsen's suggestion: "Kamloops. Alpha Four. How far is the end there?"

Al Olsen wasn't able to provide much more detail. "I don't know," he said. "I would imagine we're going to break down here against the river, and that will be it."

At 8:59, exactly 50 minutes after Al Olsen had left the RCMP Lillooet Detachment, he came in sight of Stan Walstrom and PC Twenty- Two Alpha Three. When he left Lillooet he was 23 kilometres behind, now the gap was closed. Al Olsen was right on their tail.

Stan Walstrom called in the news: "Kamloops. We have Sergeant Olsen's headlights in our view. Copy? And Michell's dash panel indicates a red light."

Al Olsen confirmed his arrival: "I see you Stan."

Watch Commander Gary Mydlak needed to know how well Al Olsen was armed. "Sergeant Olsen, Watch Commander here. You are armed with a shotgun, 10-4?"

"10-4." Replied Al Olsen, at the same time still wondering if he had the right advice on the shotgun release mechanism.

As Watch Commander Mydlak had advised Stan Walstrom earlier, the RCMP arrest procedure for a suspect known to be armed and dangerous is to order the suspect to open the door with his left hand, keep both hands in full view and exit the car. The orders, or commandments as they're called in the force, are done through the police car's loud hailer.

Stan Walstrom confirmed the procedure again with Olsen. "Al, should I get Keith to do the commandments and then keep a firearm on him if he comes out?"

"Yeah, somebody to stay with the mike, somebody else to stay with the gun."

McKay looked back at Al Olsen's rapidly approaching police cruiser. Turning to Walstrom he said, "This is good news, he must've been really moving to catch up like that." McKay paused for a minute, then said, "You know Michell has to know there's a second car behind him. In the corners, Al's car would be easy to spot."

Glancing up at Olsen's headlights in the rearview mirror, Stan Walstrom replied, "Yeah, he's not that bombed, he probably spotted Al as soon as we did."

Michell's car was slowing down again and sputtering badly. A steep hill rose directly in front of him. Clearly, his car wouldn't have the power, traction or momentum to make up the grade. This could be the end of the pursuit. Stan Walstrom was getting nervous, the tension was building, Walstrom's sentences were coming in staccato bursts.

"OK, what do you want . . . what do you want to do? . . . 'Cause he's gonna come up to this hill here, and he's not going to be able to make it . . . Cause it's pretty steep . . . and he's not going fast enough to get any speed here."

Al Olsen could sense the apprehension in Stan Walstrom's voice, kept his response short and to the point, a direct order to settle Stan Walstrom down. "Leave Keith with the mike, I'd like you with the gun."

"10-4."

The crest of the approaching hill was about six car lengths long, with a quick descent on the other side. Michell's car was stumbling as he reached the bottom of the hill. But then the motor caught, firing evenly. With more power, the car's rear tires spun on the icy road causing the green Olds to fishtail. "Shit, he's going to spin out," Stan Walstrom said to Keith McKay.

"No, look," McKay said. "He's found some gravel, this isn't over yet."

Amazingly, Michell's rear tires stopped spinning, Walstrom and McKay could see the car slow momentarily as the motor took on the load of the new-found traction, and then pick up speed. In seconds Michell topped the steep hill and kept on going. Higher and farther along the West Pavilion Road.

Kamloops Telecoms, expecting an apprehension at any minute, called Stan Walstrom. "Are you on that hill yet?"

"Yeah, 10-4. He made it all right. There were some gravel patches." The pursuit continued. But now Stan Walstrom was becoming increasingly concerned about the amount of gas he left. They were a long way out; they had no idea of the length of the road and he wanted to get this parade stopped and turned around back to Lillooet. He called Al Olsen:

"Al, we've got to get Michell stopped soon. How do you want to do this? "

Al Olsen wanted to ride it out, maintain control, with no overt moves for the moment. "I still think our best bet is to see if we can get to the dead end, no sense trying to force him."

Stan Walstrom didn't think he could make it. "My petrol, I only like, uh, have a third of a tank here and we've got a while to go before we get to any where. Kamloops, we're at the 60-kilometre mark, Sergeant Olsen's right behind me and we're approximately two and a half vehicle lengths behind the subject. All our lights are activated and the subject keeps on driving."

No one knew what was coming; but as it turned out, the pursuit of Rusty Michell would be over in eleven minutes.

8

IN THE UNITED STATES, highway patrol police officers are commonly taught to "spin and pin" a suspect's car in the course of a pursuit. In this procedure the police car comes from behind and then pulls alongside of the car to be spun. When the police car's front fender is just even with the rear tire of the evading car, the officer turns the nose of the police car into the suspect's rear fender, then hits the gas and spins the suspect's car out of control.

There are two outcomes of this technique. One, the suspect's car ends up facing backwards and is apprehended by following police cars. Or, if there is a barrier on the right side of the road, the police car is brought along slightly ahead of the rear wheels of the evading car. As the suspect's car is spun, the police car keeps pushing and pins the evading car into the side barrier. The spin and pin technique is only effective on dry surfaces where the police car has good traction.

This procedure is not taught to members of the RCMP, but Olsen thought with the slow speeds they were going, along with the advantage of having snow banks on both sides of the road, they may be able to "bump" Rusty Michell's car out of control off the road and "pin" it in a snowbank. Al Olsen asked to talk to Gary Mydlak about this course of action. "Kamloops, is the watch commander there? I'd like his opinion on whether or not we should try to tighten up our pursuit, maybe give the suspect a little nudge on one of these corners . . . we're doing 40 K's or less."

Gary Mydlak needed more information and responded by asking, "Can you tell me if, how far away from the Big Bar dead end you are?"

"No I can't. I've never been out this way. It's Al here talking, Alpha 4. We're both running half to a third of a tank of gas, travelling at 33 kilometres or less, kinda wondering if we should put an end to this, get this guy stopped."

The watch commander wasn't particularly helpful: "My map indicates that you should be very close to the Big Bar ferry dead end. I'm familiar with that area doing marijuana eradication and you should run into a dead end there."

Al Olsen thought it was a better idea to end the pursuit, before the dead end, especially since they were going slowly. They were into flatter country, plus there was a series of sweeping corners ahead where they could bring a police car along side of Rusty Michell and force his car off the road.

He called back to the communications centre, "10-4. Gary. We're gonna hang off this ride, and move the suspect around a bit."

Gary Mydlak finally seemed to understand what Al was getting at. "10-4 Al, I concur. Exercise extreme caution.

You have two members with shotguns. You've got the eyeball."

Stan Walstrom wondered who was going to do the bumping. "You gonna do that, Al?"

"Go again?"

"You gonna bump him, or am I?"

Walstrom sounded nervous, Al Olsen had second thoughts about the bumping. Maybe they should wait until the road ended. After all, if Michell kept going, time would be on their side. Michell's alcohol level would lower, he might begin to control his emotions better. If the police could keep the situation static, Michell might just stop and surrender peacefully.

Al Olsen changed his mind, telling Stan Walstrom, "No hold on, just a minute, if we're pretty sure we're really close to a dead end, we're just gonna follow him for a while."

But Stan Walstrom didn't think they were that close to the Big Bar crossing. "I thought we had, maybe some distance to go. I thought we had another 60 kilometres 'til we're out to the Big Bar."

Back in Kamloops, Gary Mydlak was trying his best figure out where they were in relationship to the end of the road. Mydlak called to Alpha Four. "Stan, can you give me some indication on your ETA at Big Bar?"

Walstrom wasn't much help. "I'm not a hundred percent familiar with this road Gary. I thought we had another 60 kilometres to go, but if we're coming to the dead end you're talking about, I don't know, I have no idea."

Mydlak tried again to get a reading on their location. "Well, on the map I've got, you should be hitting a dead end pretty soon, if I've got it figured right, following your kilometre readings. Do you have any creek markings that you can recall? Any signs like creeks . . . and which creeks?"

Stan Walstrom recalled the last sign post he'd passed. "We went over Slok Creek a while back."

Gary Mydlak hadn't heard the response clearly. "What's the name of that creek?"

"Slok." Stan Walstrom used the phonetic alphabet to spell it out. "SLOK: Sierra, Lima, Oscar, Kilo. Copy?"

Mydlak found Slok Creek on the map. Walstrom was right; they were nowhere near the Big Bar ferry. Mylak had thought Slok Creek was closer to the Big Bar ferry.

"Yeah, Alpha Three, watch commander here. I just found Slok Creek, that's way back by Pavilion. I had you way up, almost at Clinton, Big Bar area."

Listening to this, Al Olsen realized they had to end the pursuit. The Big Bar dead end was a long way away. They were running out of gas. They were getting too far into the mountains and away from RCMP support. He had to make a decision. He called Stan Walstrom: "Stan we're only half way, about 64 kilometres I think. Stan?"

Walstrom replied, "10-4."

"OK Stan. We're going to look for a place to stop him here. You ready?"

"10-4.

Al Olsen spoke slowly saying, "I want you to look for a sweeper corner to the left. Get behind him and give him a nudge." Just then the Olds slowed, they could hear the big V-8 motor hesitating and running roughly again. This could be it. Then the engine caught and the car lurched forward, the rear end sliding to the right, tires spinning on the compacted snow.

Olsen called Walstrom: "I thought we had a stop there for a minute, Stan."

Walstrom replied, he was tense, "Yeah, my heart was pumping there. Either he's going to run out of fuel, or I'm going to. He's going a little faster on this corner, here."

Stan Walstrom relaxed a bit, his next transmission was more like a friendly chat; he was trying to lighten up, somehow play down the tension.

"Kamloops we're just coming up to the 65 kilometre mark, copy that? We have extreme winter conditions and no-o-o gravel on the road. If he stops, Al, I'll go on his side with my vehicle and you go Keith's side. Copy?"

"10-4."

Suddenly Gary Mydlak's voice boomed in their ears: "Alpha Three, Alpha Four, we have information that Big Bar ferry is approximately 100 kilometres from Lillooet."

Both police cars had just passed the 65 kilometre mark. Al Olsen knew then that they had to get Rusty Michell stopped. He called Stan Walstrom. "Hey, we're not going that far. We don't have enough fuel for that. We're going to stop this guy now. If we go further, I don't think we have any chance of getting out of here and back to Lillooet."

Stan Walstrom agreed. They had to stop Michell now. He called Al Olsen for advice: "Should we bump him?"

As they approached the 66 kilometre mark, Olsen could see the road was flattening out, but was still twisting. Because of the extreme ice, Michell would have to slow down in the corners. In a left-turning corner, it would be possible for Stan Walstrom to get behind Rusty Michell's car and push him into the snowbank on the right side of the road. If Walstrom could pull this off, Michell's car would be in the ditch. Stan's car would be up blocking the driver's side door of the Olds and the passenger's side door would be up tight against the snowbank.

Al Olsen set up the maneuver for Stan Walstrom. "We want to force him into a corner where we have him on the right hand side. It's very slow here. Go ahead and take him out on the right hand side. He's not giving up. We want to do him . . . get him on a corner if we can, because he's about down to 10 kilometres an hour, if we can just push him sideways."

Walstrom responded: "10-4. We want to have him on the inside corner, though."

In all police operations where it's expected that shots will be fired, having an unobstructed field of vision and field of fire is critical. Al Olsen had to ensure that if Michell's car was off the road, it was off to the right. This would mean Rusty Michell, in the left-side driver's seat, would be visible from the road.

"10-4. It'll also give us both a better field, and it's the safest way to bring it to quick ending."

Stan Walstrom stayed right on Michell's tail waiting for him to slow while in a sweeping left-hand corner. He saw an opening for a bump. "Right here, Al?"

"Right here if he slows down."

Suddenly, Michell hit the accelerator, picking up speed. Stan Walstrom's police car was getting too close. Michell must have suspected they were trying to force him off the road. Stan Walstrom was upset; he'd missed a good opportunity to take Michell out on the corner.

"No good." He said.

Al Olsen responded: "No sweat. We've got lots of time to do it, we'll pick the one we want."

As Walstrom approached the 67-kilometre sign, he saw the corner he was looking for. The road was on a slight downgrade, and they were approaching the bottom of a sweeping "s" turn to the left. Stan Walstrom hit the gas pedal, picking up speed and aiming his front bumper squarely at the left rear bumper of Michell's Oldsmobile. Walstrom was doing 40 kilometres an hour when PC Twenty-Two Alpha Three smashed into the back of the big Olds, sending it straight ahead through the corner and into the ditch on the right-hand side of the road.

It was exactly what Stan Walstrom had wanted to happen. But to his amazement, Michell yanked the steering around to the left, floored the accelerator pedal and drove back onto the road, wheels spinning, snow flying, but out of the ditch and under control. Stan Walstrom couldn't believe what he'd seen. Michell was probably still so drunk he couldn't walk, but he'd managed to keep his car on the road after being forced into the ditch at 40 kilometres an hour.

Michell was back on the road. At the middle of the "s" turn there was a right-hand corner coming, Walstrom gunned the police car engine and hit Michell's rear bumper again. Once more the green Olds went straight ahead, this time hitting the snow bank on the left-hand side of the road. But again Michell turned out the snowbank, buried the gas pedal and drove back on to the road.

"Geez, I don't believe it," Walstrom said to an equally amazed Keith McKay, "he's recovered again."

Keith McKay smiled, Michell's good luck was incredible. "Yeah, he's some sort of driver all right."

"Not this time, dammit," Walstrom said.

Now at the top of the "s" turn, he gunned the police car's 5.0 liter V-8, his snow tires spun on the icy logging road. He hit Michell's car on the right-hand side of the rear bumper. Walstrom's speedometer was reading 38 kilometres an hour when he rammed into the green Oldsmobile for the third time. Again, Michell's car headed

Top: *An aerial view of the "s" turn.*
Above: *The "s" turn.*

into the snow bank on the left-hand side, he spun the steering wheel to the right, hit the gas, drove out of the ditch and kept on going down the road.

But then the unexpected happened. Walstrom had hit his gas pedal too hard, and he went into an uncontrollable spin. The rear end of the police car was skidding around to the right. Walstrom tried to steer into the spin and recover, but it was too icy. PC Twenty-Two Alpha Three was doing a 180 degree pirouette down the West Pavilion logging road. The police car hit the ditch backwards. It ended up completely off the road, buried up to its axles in snow and out of commission.

Olsen, right behind Walstrom, saw how deep Stan's car was in the snow bank. "God, this has got be the worst possible situation I could be in," he said to himself. "He's got me trapped, there's bugger-all I can do except stay on his tail. This is the shits."

Since he didn't dare let Michell out of his sight, he couldn't stop to help Stan and Keith. Olsen had to stay right on top of Michell and with no chance of backup, get Michell stopped and under control before he had a chance to use his rifle.

Walstrom and McKay watched Al Olsen speed by. "God, you're on own, Al," Stan muttered.

Stan tried to drive the car out of the snowbank. It wasn't moving. Stan turned to Keith and said, "OK you get behind the wheel, I'll get to the back and push, and let's see if we can rock the car out."

"OK," Keith replied. But he didn't think it would work. The car was buried too deeply.

Stan quickly got out of his snow bound police car. McKay sat in behind the wheel and tried to drive it out of the snow bank while Stan Walstrom pushed. A few hundred metres down the road, Olsen picked up speed. Now, all alone, it was absolutely critical to keep Rusty Michell in sight. He called Kamloops.

"Kamloops, Alpha Four, I'm still here, I think Stan got stuck."

At the 67.5 kilometre area the West Pavilion Road begins a slight downgrade and takes a bit of a sweep to the right. Michell hit this stretch with too much speed. He tried to slow down, it was too late. The rear end of the Oldsmobile began to slide out to the left with the nose pointing in to the right-hand side ditch. Amazingly, Michell had the presence of mind to attempt to correct the slide. He attempted to steer into the skid, but this time Michell couldn't pull out of the slide.

The road surface was absolutely slick, there was no traction, Rusty Michell's Oldsmobile plowed into the left snow bank and shuddered to a stop. But, the car's right rear fender was sticking well into the middle of the road.

Al Olsen was right behind Michell. He came around the corner. Suddenly he could see the green Oldsmobile, stopped and angled across the road. The right front end in the snow bank with the right rear fender well into the driving lane of the icy mountain road. Olsen cursed, thinking, shit he's stopped, right in the centre of the friggin' road. Christ, I'm going to run into him.

Al Olsen hit his brakes, then tried pumping them to gain traction, but the road was far too slippery. His car skidded, there was no way he could avoid hitting Michell's car. All he could think about was doing as little as damage as possible to the police car. Olsen's car police car hit the right rear corner of the Oldsmobile's wrap-around bumper, damaging the left side of the police car's grille. Both cars were stopped. What now?

Top and Above: *The bump and pin manoeuvre.*

The bump and pin manoeuvre.

Suddenly, Al Olsen stiffened. Rusty Michell was out of his car! He was standing at the back of the Oldsmobile, no more than a metre away from Al Olsen looking at the damage to the back of the Oldsmobile. He had his .303 Lee Enfield rifle in his hand!

"Oh fuck," Al said to himself, "I'm dead." He ducked down to the right, trying to find cover behind the police car dashboard. He grabbed for the Remington 12-gauge shotgun. He hit the release button, remembering Walstrom had told him it was the one on the far right. He heard the electric lock mechanism open, he'd found the right control. He pulled at the gun. "Goddammit," he swore, the shotgun wouldn't come out! Because Al Olsen was crouched over, he wasn't pulling straight up on the gun stock and the shotgun wouldn't come out of its U-shaped holder.

Al looked up. He was in a terrifying and deadly situation. Michell had moved from the front of the police car to within feet of Olsen and his side window. He was in a violent mood, screaming and yelling at Al Olsen, his face was ugly and contorted, even through the police car's rolled up window, Al Olsen could hear Michell screaming at him.

"I'm going to fucking kill you, kill you. You fucking asshole! Fucking cops!" Then Michell moved closer to the police car, he was now less than a metre away from the car door, his rifle raised!

Al was still leaning down to his right. He hit the gun-release switch again and pulled at the shotgun. It still wouldn't come out! Michell's rifle was now raised and pointed directly down at him! Olsen grabbed his Smith and Wesson service revolver which was still laying on the police car passenger seat. His window was up, but there was no time to roll it down, all Al could think of was to fire five rapid shots. Just five. Save one round, in case the first shots missed.

He leaned back towards the middle of the seat, took the two-handed grip on the Police Special .38, aimed up through the driver's side window at the armed Rusty Michell and started firing.

Al Olsen's first shot hit Rusty Michell's raised left arm just above the wrist. The 158 grain .38 hollow-point bullet broke Michell's radial bone, then split into fragments. One larger piece of the fragmented bullet hit Rusty in the chest, causing a superficial skin wound just above his left nipple. The shot to the wrist spun Rusty Michell around. His back was now towards the police car. Olsen couldn't see a thing. The tempered side window glass had shattered at the first shot, creating an opaque screen.

His second shot completely blew out the shattered window and caught Rusty Michell in the lower right of his back, it hit his right pelvis bone and deflected inward towards the chest wall. This shot dropped Rusty to his hands and knees at the side of the road. Al Olsen kept firing. Shots three, four and five missed, going well over the head of the now-fallen Rusty Michell.

Olsen had one more round left. He sat up and looked out the shattered police car window. Rusty Michell was on his hands and knees, still hanging on to the .303 Lee Enfield. He was getting to his feet!

Olsen had no idea if he'd wounded Michell or not. Still holding his revolver in the two-handed position, he sat up, pointed his gun out the shattered window, cutting his left hand on the broken window glass in the process, and fired his final round. The last shot hit Rusty in the left lower back. Because Michell was on his hands and knees, his torso parallel to the ground, the bullet proceeded up through Michell's body.

This was the fatal wound. The hollow-point bullet ripped through Michell's left kidney, passed though the diaphragm muscle, then through the base of the heart, it tore the right upper lobe of the lung and finally lodged in the front of the chest wall, close to Michell's right shoulder. The wound to the heart resulted in an immediate and substantial blood loss. Within minutes Rusty Michell would be dead.

Al Olsen got on the radio, his voice was shaking, he was hyperventilating. "Kamloops, we now have shots fired. I need an ambulance. Stan, I am not injured, the other guy is. He came at me with a rifle, I need assistance, as fast as I can get it."

Kamloops responded: "10-4."

Al Olsen continued, he was emotionally devastated; he had to talk it out: "I hit him more than once. I don't know how many times. I don't know what his condition is. Stan, I'm just a few hundred yards past where you are. I came around the corner, he braked it on me and stopped. He jumped out with a rifle. Fuck I thought I was dead."

Al Olsen was shaking. He got out of the car, his service revolver still in his hand, Rusty Michell was on his stomach, the Lee Enfield rifle underneath him, he was alive, and amazingly, considering his extensive injuries, was still trying to stand up.

Olsen realized his revolver was empty. He tossed it on the front seat of his car, reached in the car and hit the shotgun release button. Pulling straight up from this position, the shotgun came out easily. Al Olsen had to secure the Lee Enfield rifle, he had no idea of the extent of Michell's injuries, but he did know that if the downed man was faking it, he could still get a shot off.

By this time, Walstrom and McKay, guns drawn, were running from their ditched police car and rapidly heading up the road towards Al Olsen. As they came on the shooting scene, 500 metres from where their car had gone off the road, they could see Al Olsen's car up against the rear bumper of the Oldsmobile. Rusty Michell was on the ground a metre from the driver's side door of the police car. He was face down, legs on the roadway, laying in the snowbank at the edge of the road. He was writhing on the ground, trying to get his breath.

Al Olsen was standing over Rusty Michell, pointing the Remington shotgun at him. Olsen was screaming, "Drop the rifle and roll over. Now! Roll over slowly and let go of the rifle, let go of the rifle!"

It was clear, Al Olsen was terribly shaken, he kept screaming at Rusty Michell to let go of the gun and roll over.

Michell rolled over slowly, there was blood on the ground from the bullet he'd taken in the wrist. In the snow, alongside the bloodstain, lay the Lee Enfield rifle. For Rusty Michell, the Christmas Eve chase 67.5 kilometres along the West Pavilion Road was over, and in a few more minutes he would die. For Sergeant Al Olsen, the Rusty Michell incident was just beginning.

9

When Rusty Michell rolled over, the three officers could see he was seriously wounded. His breathing was labored, he was struggling to move but going nowhere.

"This isn't good," said Al Olsen. "Yeah," Stan Walstrom replied.

"OK," Al said. "Let's move him into a three-quarter prone, maybe it'll help him breath easier. Keith, pop the trunk in my car and get the emergency blanket."

As they covered Rusty Michell and moved him on to his side, Stan Walstrom picked up Michell's rifle, closed the trunk lid and put the rifle on top of the trunk of Al Olsen's police car. They could see the clear outline of the old Lee Enfield in the snow where Rusty had fallen on it.

Once again, Watch Commander Gary Mydlak's big voice came barking over the police car radio. "OK, what is the last kilometre reading you have?"

Still shaking, from the events of the shooting, Olsen replied, "We're around . . . past the 65 kilometre I believe. Send two tow trucks when you send the ambulance."

Kamloops confirmed the request. "Two tow trucks, 10-4."

Al Olsen couldn't concentrate, his thoughts raced. He clicked on the mike again, he was still shaking. "Cancel one. We can get Stan's car out. No . . . . might as well send two, I don't know if my vehicle's even driveable."

As watch commander, Corporal Gary Mydlak had a responsibility for maintaining the integrity of the shooting scene. He needed an update. "We copy, Alpha Three, confirm please if the weapon is secure and all members are OK."

Stan Walstrom responded immediately, his voice shaking. "10-4, all members are fine, copy? All members are safe and secure. Subject has been attended to and . . . we need an ambulance out here . . . like ten minutes ago."

RCMP regulations required that Gary Mydlak have an officer at the scene confirm that Michell's gun was secure. Mydlak had to report the shooting up the RCMP command ladder as quickly as he could and the first question he'd be asked, would be to confirm that all weapons were secure. So once again Mydlak asked about the gun.

"10-4 we copy. Secure the suspect's weapon and respond please."

Gary Mydlak's last query was lost on Walstrom. He was concentrating on Rusty Michell. Stan Walstrom could see that Michell's vital signs were fading. Keith McKay bent over the fallen Michell and checked for a pulse, it was still there, but Michell's increasingly labored breathing and distorted facial features were not good signs.

RCMP regulations require a senior NCO to attend at a fatal shooting scene; Stan Walstrom knew by now he was watching Rusty Michell die.

It was a distressing sight, Michell's baseball cap was on the ground next to his right shoulder. His eyes were partly open, his breathing was heavy and slowing. In his struggle to breathe, Michell's mouth was open. Stan Walstrom could see that Michell had three upper front teeth missing. His shirt had pulled out at the waist, his midriff was bare, and his right hand held a handful of some snow he must have involuntarily grabbed when the last and fatal bullet hit him.

Stan Walstrom pulled the emergency blanket back, as he did this he could see a small blood-stained tear in the left breast area of Rusty Michell's pullover style jacket. He zipped open the top part of the jacket to reveal the blood-covered hole in Rusty's T-shirt. Stan Walstrom walked back to the police car and called back to Watch Commander Mydlak.

"Kamloops, can we have a Section NCO come out this way. It . . . it doesn't look like the shooting victim's going to survive. He has one entry above the nipple area and he's . . . his eyes are all rolled back and he's . . . he smells strongly of alcohol and he has a white foam around his mouth. Copy?"

Gary Mydlak was more concerned about the rifle than Michell's rapidly worsening condition. "Alpha Three, Kamloops. OK Alpha Three. Watch Commander here. Please confirm the suspect's weapon is secured and I'll be on the phone as soon as you confirm that to the commanding officer."

"10-4, Kamloops. Subject had a rifle, it was three feet from where he uh . . . landed, he's down on his back right now. Sergeant Olsen has checked him and Olsen is now checking the vehicle. Copy?"

Al Olsen walked over to the green Olds and looked in the driver's side. What he saw said it all. On the seat were two cans of beer, a flash light and one glove, the other glove was on the ground just outside the door of the car. On the floor of the car, lay two packs of Export A cigarettes, the empty magazine for the Lee Enfield rifle and five .303 rounds.

Olsen could see that Michell couldn't have had the magazine properly clipped in to the rifle. As he jumped out of the car Michell must have hit the clip against the steering wheel, knocking it out of the rifle and on to the floor. Once out of the rifle, the spring-loaded magazine spewed its bullets out on the car floor.

Olsen ran back to his car where Michell's Lee Enfield rifle was laying on the police car's trunk deck. He looked at the bottom opening where the Lee Enfield magazine would clip in the rifle, then he lifted he bolt, pulled it back and opened the bolt-action rifle. It was like taking a sickening kick in the gut. Rusty Michell had come at him with an empty rifle! He had shot an unarmed man! But, how could he have known the gun was unloaded?

This was the Pinchie shooting all over again. Another Indian, pointing a rifle at an armed police officer. Too drunk to know the gun wasn't loaded. Another senseless shooting. Probably another man dead.

Al Olsen put the rifle back on the trunk his car, then walked back to look at Rusty Michell. Keith McKay, who was standing over the dying man, heard Olsen say, "No, no, not again, not again."

Gary Mydlak continued to ask about securing Michell's rifle. "Alpha Three, as soon as you confirm you have the suspect's weapon secured, I'll be contacting the Commanding Officer. Copy?"

"10-4, Watch Commander. Copy."

RCMP regulations state that an officer who has shot a person is treated as a suspect in that shooting. Still visibly shaken, Olsen took his revolver from the front seat of the car, handed it to Stan Walstrom and explained the RCMP administrative procedures to the young Constable. "Stan, I'm technically your boss . . . uh, but I'm also to be considered a suspect. I was involved . . . I'm the shooter in this case. You have to take charge of the scene and the exhibits. You have to treat me as the suspect in the case . . . You must be sure to take proper notes and record our conversations . . . Anything that would be pertinent to the case must be written down." Al paused, he was still trying to catch his breath, then he continued, "I was still in my car . . . he came at me with his rifle in the firing position. As you can see . . . I shot at him through the police car window. I fired all six rounds."

Stan Walstrom flipped the revolver's cylinder open. The primers on all six shells bore the indent where they'd been hit by the firing pin. They indentations were all off-centre, indicating a well-worn cylinder mechanism action being fired too quickly for the shells to line up right on centre with the firing pin.

Walstrom called Mydlak with the information on Olsen's gun. He was quick to describe the events and the self-defence action taken by Al Olsen. "Just to advise . . . just inspected Sergeant Olsen's service revolver. All six rounds are discharged, he'd had his sidearm on his seat when the subject approached the PC . . . He had to shoot through his window to hit the subject . . . as the subject was approaching with a rifle."

Stan Walstrom put the empty revolver back on the front seat of Al Olsen's car. He took Rusty Michell's Lee

Top: *Twenty-two Alpha Four with shattered window.*
Above: *The shattered window glass and Al Olsen's .38*
Police Special on the front seat.

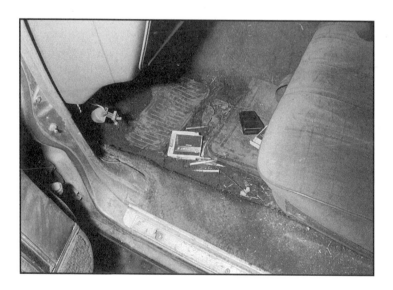

Top: *Olsen's revolver, showing all six rounds fired.*
Above: *The floor of the green Oldsmobile, with the Lee Enfield rifle magazine and the .303 rounds on the floor.*

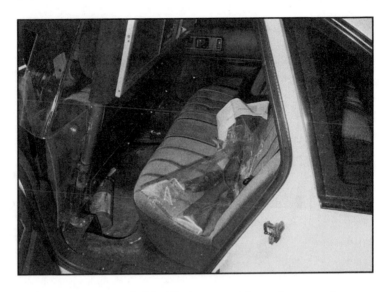

Rusty's Lee Enfield rifle in an evidence bag on the back seat of Twenty-two Alpha Four.

Enfield from the trunk lid of the police car and put the rifle in an evidence bag. He placed the evidence bag in the back seat of Al Olsen's car.

It was a chilling scene. Rusty Michell's heavily labored breathing was slowing, they knew they were watching him die. Mydlak called again. "Alpha Three. Watch Commander here, I want you to confirm . . . and acknowledge my broadcast, to secure the suspect's firearm and confirm that please, the suspect's firearm is secure."

Stan Walstrom responded. "That is confirmed, copy that is confirmed."

McKay continued to check Michell's vital signs, twice he checked the carotid artery on Michell's neck and found a pulse. But when he checked a third time, there was no pulse. Rusty Michell was gone. A victim of his own anger. "He's dead," McKay said simply.

The time of death was 9:37 p.m. less than two hours after Kathy James had first called the RCMP asking for their assistance.

All rural police cars carry a 35mm camera for accident and crime scene photos and Walstrom got the camera out of Olsen's car and began taking shots of the scene. He noted that there were no skid marks on the road leading up to the point where Michell's car had hit the ditch. He called out to McKay and Olsen, saying, "Hey, you know he must have driven right into the snowbank, or maybe he thought he could drive through it. Whatever he was thinking, he sure as hell wasn't trying to stop."

Keith McKay walked over the side of the car to have a look. "Yeah," he said. "Either that, or he used the snowbank as a fast way to stop and force Al's hand." Keith looked over at the right fender of the Oldsmobile, it was really buried. He shivered, he'd only been wearing a light jacket when he'd answered Walstrom's call for assistance earlier that evening. "It's cold up here," he said.

"Yeah," Walstrom agreed. "Listen, go sit in Al's car, but I'm going to keep shooting photos and taking notes, the internal investigation coming out of this is going to be brutal." Keith McKay got into Al Olsen's car, it was warm, the motor was still running, there was enough gas in the tank to let the car's engine idle until the tow truck arrived.

Al Olsen was still pacing, he looked at Michell, whose eyes were partly open, his mouth was agape and even dead he seemed to be mocking the police. Al shivered and turned away, all he could only think of what lay ahead. Sure as hell, he thought to himself, the native community is going to be on my case. He'd seen their reaction at Pinchie and this shooting would no different. Another major setback for RCMP/aboriginal relations.

On top of the native problem, Al Olsen would soon face the two-stage RCMP statute investigation. At the subdivision level, there would be an intensive investigation to determine if the cause of death was the result of a criminal action. A thorough examination would be carried out, and even Al Olsen's clothes would be seized for forensic analysis.

At the same time, a second separate investigation would be undertaken by an officer from RCMP E Division headquarters in Vancouver to establish if proper operating procedures and force policy had been followed in the shooting of Michell. The evidence and reports from both RCMP investigations would then be sent to provincial Crown Council for their review. It would be up to Crown Council to recommend whether or not charges be laid against Al Olsen. The thrust of Crown Council's investigation would be to determine if Al Olsen had shot Rusty Michell in self defence.

10

EVEN BEFORE RUSTY MICHELL DIED, Kathy James knew something dreadful had happened. Wayne Redan had called her to tell her about the shooting. He'd heard Olsen's description of the shots he'd fired and sensed the panic in Olsen's voice.

Wayne told Kathy, "Normally when cops talk on the radio it's pretty boring," he told Kathy. "But this guy was really shitting his pants. Like he was awful nervous and kinda running out of breath when he spoke. He said shots were fired and the other guy needed an ambulance. We heard them say Rusty's name on the scanner."

Kathy was panicking and quickly asked, "What did they say about Russell?"

Wayne's response was not what Kathy wanted to hear. "I gotta figure Rusty's been shot, and the way the other cop talked about Rusty, with his eyes rolled back and foam coming out of his mouth and everything, I think they killed him."

Kathy James called the RCMP immediately, but the Telecoms operator would tell her only that there was no one available at the Lillooet detachment, that an officer would talk to her as quickly as possible. She kept calling, demanding to know what happened to Rusty. The answer was the same: "There is no one available at the Lillooet detachment, but an officer will speak to you in person as soon as possible."

It would be eight hours before the RCMP would tell Kathy James that her common-law husband of nine years had been shot and killed at 9:37 the previous evening, 67.5 kilometres away from the Bridge River Reserve on the West Pavilion Road.

At the RCMP Kamloops Subdivision headquarters, things were happening quickly. The acting officer in charge that evening was Inspector Peter Netherway. Watch Commander Gary Mydlak called Netherway and gave him a full report of the Michell shooting. The Inspector immediately called Staff Sergeant G. "Harry" Danyluk, East Section NCO of the Kamloops subdivision, and advised him that he would be in charge of the statute investigation. Danyluk would be assisted by Sergeant Earl Shockey, who was in charge of the Subdivision General Investigation Section. Danyluk lived east of Kamloops in Chase BC, and Shockey lived close to Danyluk on the north shore of Little Shuswap Lake.

Earl Shockey picked up Harry Danyluk at a few minutes past 10:00 p.m. and they left for the long four-and-a-half hour drive to the shooting scene on West Pavilion Road. They both agreed it was a hell of a way to spend Christmas Eve.

"Boy, this is a tough one," Harry Danyluk said to Earl Shockey. "We've got three policemen there at the scene, they all have to be investigated."

Danyluk had to have the shooting scene secured. He called Kamloops Telecoms. "Kamloops, Staff Sergeant Danyluk here. If there's anyone left around the detachment, I need the most senior man left in Lillooet to take over, seize all exhibits and make sure the scene at the West Pavilion Road shooting stays uncontaminated until I arrive." Danyluk thought for a moment then added, "Have the watch commander arrange for a photo ident officer, a critical incident member, and have someone contact the local coroner."

Kamloops responded, "10-4."

RCMP Constable Joe dePaulo was dispatched from Lillooet in accordance with Staff Sergeant Danyluk's instructions.

At 11:32 p.m. the ambulance arrived at kilometre 67.5. Because gun shot wounds had been reported, Marie Vidal, an attendant with an EMA-2 rating, an advanced degree of ambulance-attendant training, had been called out to make the trip out the West Pavilion Road. Vidal was accompanied by ambulance attendants Dana Yaremchuk and Shannon Dubroy.

Vidal did an obligatory check of Rusty Michell for vital signs, looking for a pulse, heart, or lung sounds; there were none. Michell had been dead for two hours.

Al Olsen had to have the back of his hand attended to, and he joined Marie Vidal in the back of the ambulance.

"How are you doing?" Vidal asked as attendant Dubroy cleaned and bandaged the back of Olsen's hand.

"God I'm wiped." Al Olsen replied. He was still shaking, his breathing quickened by the shock of the shooting. "This was tough, he just came at me, he was coming at me outside my car window. He was pointing a rifle at me, I figured I was dead. All I could think of was my wife and kids, everything flashed by. All I could think to do was empty my gun at him."

Shortly after, Marie Vidal, Dana Yaremchuk and Shannon Dubroy left the scene to return to Lillooet. Rusty Michell's body remained where he had fallen in the snowbank, awaiting RCMP identification officer Constable Bill Pound, Constable Joe dePaulo and Staff Sergeant Danyluk.

Pound and dePaulo along with RCMP Auxiliary Cst. Bob Rankin were next on the scene. Bill Pound immediately got to work on the identification procedures, photographing, then videotaping every relevant detail. Bill Pound took 34 still photos of the shooting scene that winter morning, all of which would play a vital role in the RCMP investigation and the subsequent coroner's inquest. At 2:30 in the a.m., Harry Danyluk and Earl Shockey arrived at kilometre 67.5 on the West Pavilion Road. They had passed the returning ambulance thirty minutes earlier.

Olsen went over to talk to Harry Danyluk. Danyluk was firm on the rules of a Criminal Code statute investigation. He advised Olsen of the procedure he was going to follow.

"Sergeant Olsen, I have to advise you not to speak to me, nor will I speak to you until such time as I have inspected the scene. After I have examined the scene, I will speak to you, but only in accordance with the rules of a statute investigation." Harry Danyluk gave the same advice to Keith McKay and Stan Walstrom.

Danyluk waited for Pound to finish photographing the scene. Then he did a walk around, noted Michell's rifle in the plastic bag on the seat of the police car and Olsen's service revolver on the glass covered driver's seat of the car. He stopped to look at Rusty Michell's body. Pound

Top: *The bullet trajectories fired from Al Olsen's revolver.*
Above: *The bullet trajectories viewed from the source.*

was still taking photos of Michell and Harry Danyluk did not examine the fallen man closely, except to note that the small hole in the upper left nipple area. Harry Danyluk didn't think this was the fatal wound.

At 2:50 a.m. BC Government Agent Bob Hall arrived with RCMP Sergeant Bob Leach, who represented the RCMP member's assistance program. Hall was also the Lillooet coroner.

Danyluk continued his on-site investigation. Everything was in order, but with three officers involved at the shooting, there was going to be a lot of paperwork to do.

Harry Danyluk left the scene well after four in the morning. Rusty Michell's body was put into a body bag and loaded into an RCMP Chevy Blazer for transport to the Lillooet Funeral Home. Later on that day, Joe dePaulo took Rusty Michell's remains to Royal Inland Hospital morgue at Kamloops where an autopsy would be done two days later, on December 27.

Then Danyluk instructed the local officers to have Telecoms contact Rusty Michell's immediate family and get them down to the Lillooet RCMP detachment. As senior officer on the investigation, Staff Sergeant Harry Danyluk would take responsibility for personally telling Kathy James that her husband was dead.

11

IT WAS NOW CLOSE TO FIVE O'CLOCK in the morning, Christmas Day. Kathy James was frantic. She had been calling the Lillooet RCMP detachment for hours, but with all available officers responding to the shooting, her calls were being transferred to Kamloops Telecoms. The communications operators, following RCMP procedure, which prohibits providing this type of information by telephone, would tell Kathy Michell only that someone would be coming to talk to her.

In desperation, Kathy decided to drive up the West Pavilion Road and find out for herself what had happened. She and three friends left her home on the Bridge River Reserve shortly after five a.m. It was still dark.

At kilometre 20, Kathy met the police cars on their way back to town. Stan Walstrom's car had been pulled from the ditch and Al Olsen's was still driveable. With all the RCMP officials who had attended the scene at kilometre 67.5, a large contingent was returning to Lillooet. Kathy had no way of knowing that Rusty Michell was in a body bag in Joe dePaulo's RCMP Chevrolet Blazer. But she knew something was terribly wrong, because the green Oldsmobile was being pulled by a tow truck.

The RCMP stopped briefly and an officer talked to one of Kathy's companions and advised him that they should all return to Lillooet and that Kathy should go to the RCMP detachment where Staff Sergeant Danyluk would talk to her.

Kathy arrived at the Main Street detachment in Lillooet a few minutes after 6 a.m. Harry Danyluk took her into Al Olsen's corner office and told her that her husband, Russell Michell, had been fatally shot the previous evening by a member of the RCMP.

For Kathy James, listening to Harry Danyluk calmly and slowly describe the circumstances surrounding Rusty's death was like living a bad dream, yet she was wide awake and knew that Harry was only confirming what she had sensed for hours.

Harry didn't mince words, nor did he try to patronize Kathy James. He simply told her what had happened. Hearing Harry Danyluk's openly sympathetic, yet straightforward account of the shooting only made Rusty's death more difficult for Kathy to take. She couldn't be angry with Harry Danyluk, who was only doing what he had to do.

There was no going back to the last time she'd seen Rusty alive. There was nothing to do, nothing left to say, no second chances. Russell Michell, her common-law husband, the father of four of her children was dead. Kathy would never see him, nor talk with him again. He would never take the kids fishing again; he would never play music with the guys at the Fountain Reserve.

She went through the whole range of emotions that comes when the mind tries to work its way through distress. First she blamed herself for phoning the RCMP. Then she blamed the RCMP. Finally, the emotional realization of her loss took over, driving her back to reality. There is no one to blame, only Russell to grieve, Russell was gone, leaving only his spirit to be mourned.

Kathy James left the RCMP detachment at a few minutes past 6:30 Christmas Day morning. She was heartbroken, tired and emotionally exhausted. She had first called the RCMP at 7:42 the previous evening, at the time desperately in need of protection from Russell Michell. Now eleven hours later, all she wanted was to have Russell home and alive.

Al Olsen drove back to town with Sergeant Bob Leach from the RCMP members assistance program. It was a tough, yet calming trip. Tough, because Al knew what was coming in the next months both in terms of the two-stage RCMP investigation and the crown prosecutor's report. There was more though, Al knew the moody anger that would soon begin to smolder on the Indian reserves and on the streets of Lillooet.

After Hugh Malone had shot Randy Monk on the Pinchie Reserve, Al had seen the way sullen mistrust and brooding could fester in the native community. Sure as hell, he thought, it would be the same all over again in Lillooet.

But the trip back was also calming, simply because it took so long and gave Al a chance to talk it out with Bob Leach. Bob was skilled at what psychologists call critical incident stress debriefing. It was important for Al to have the support and the companionship of a colleague, a reason why the RCMP assigns fellow officers to handle stressful situations.

The Michell pursuit had been particularly troubling for Al Olsen. It was long, close to two hours. The mind can't take much more than four hours of intense stress. Also, what preyed on him was that he had been unable to control the pursuit and apprehend Rusty Michell peacefully.

Ironically, police officers, and others who work in emergency or stressful-response situations, are trained to take and maintain control. When something goes wrong and they lose control, they sense failure. This is what bothered Al Olsen. Although he couldn't have called off the pursuit, he couldn't help but think that he shouldn't have allowed it to end the way it did.

As Al Olsen returned along the same icy West Pavilion Road he'd driven so quickly just hours earlier, he became very aware of icy and dangerous driving conditions. He couldn't really remember any specific details about the road from his trip up, but now, coming back down, it seemed so awfully narrow and with no guard rails, so unsafe.

Al Olsen and Bob Leach had left the scene of the shooting an hour before the rest of the investigating team and arrived in Lillooet at five in the morning. They went to the RCMP detachment office, where Al spent a few minutes, then went home.

He tried to sleep, it was fitful. At 10:00 a.m. Al returned to the police station and spent two hours going over Rusty Michell's death with investigating officer Earl Shockey.

At 1:00 p.m. Al returned home. There he experienced one of the truly kind things that happens in a police force as large but still as close as the RCMP.

Frank Pitts, an RCMP member who had served with Al Olsen in Fort St. James and was now stationed in 100 Mile House, two hours north of Lillooet, had heard about the Michell shooting and Al Olsen's involvement. Pitts knew what Al and Joan Olsen would be going through, so he drove down to Lillooet with his wife and family, bringing a turkey dinner and all the trimmings.

It was exactly what the Olsen family needed: a Christmas meal surrounded by friendly faces to help them take their minds off the tragic events of just a few hours earlier. It was a good evening.

The next day, Al Olsen, wife Joan and sons Brad and Chad left for Kelowna where they would spend a day and a half with Joan's family. It was a welcome and much needed time-out for the family. Al knew the mood was going to turn ugly in Lillooet, and he was right. They returned to Lillooet the evening of December 27.

Also on December 27, at 10:00 in the morning, Dr. J.D. McNaughton, a Kamloops pathologist, performed the autopsy on Russell Michell at the Royal Inland Hospital morgue in Kamloops. RCMP identification officer Bill Pound took photographs of the autopsy. In attendance, as well, was Chief Coroner Bob Graham and Brian Rasmussen, a former RCMP officer and now a member of Graham's staff.

Dr. McNaughton's report described the three bullet wounds and concluded with the following comments. "A third gunshot wound entered the left lower back and through a superior or cephalad course [moving towards the head] it passed through the heart and the right lung to its final resting location just beneath the skin on the anterior upper chest wall adjacent to the right shoulder."

Dr. McNaughton's clinical report continued, in three sentences describing an event that took only a fraction of a second to happen, yet irretrievably ended Russell Michell's 31-year-old life. Describing the third and fatal shot, Dr. McNaughton wrote; "This particular gunshot wound was the most significant in terms of death. It passed through the heart resulting in substantial blood loss with hemopericardium (an effusion of blood within the sac enclosing the heart) and a right hemothorax (a collection of blood in the lungs). Death is attributed to the blood loss as a result of this gunshot wound." At the time of death, Rusty Michell's blood alcohol count was 0.21, close to three times the legal limit.

On December 28, Rusty Michell's body was returned to Lillooet and on December 30, he was buried at the reserve cemetery. His funeral was attended by hundreds of mourners. In death, Russell Michell would have a profound and lingering impact on the Lillooet native and non-native community.

12

THE RCMP HAS A PROUD HISTORY as Canada's national police force. First called the North West Mounted Police, the Mounties established a first-class reputation as law and order was brought to the Canadian West.

When it comes to publicly celebrating its high profile, the RCMP is second to none. The red serge dress uniform is recognized all over the world, along with the internationally acclaimed RCMP musical ride, a dazzling display of horsemanship that's thrilled millions of spectators over the years. However, when it comes to operational procedures, the RCMP had always taken the position that the less the public knew, the better. And as a national force, the RCMP had been able to distance itself from the type of public scrutiny that commonly faces municipal police forces. In the Russell Michell shooting, though, that inward-looking paramilitary attitude would change, and for the first time, the RCMP would be immediately front and centre with the details.

Within hours of reviewing the circumstances of Rusty Michell's death, Superintendent Len Olfert, Commanding

Officer of the RCMP Kamloops Subdivision knew that unless he acted quickly, he, and the force would be caught up in a public relations disaster. Len Olfert could just see the headlines now, "Unarmed Lillooet Indian man, shot twice in the back by senior RCMP officer."

There was too much at stake here. Al Olsen's career could be ruined and there was no way that Len Olfert could allow that to happen. Olsen was a good officer, with sound judgment and a solid, twenty-one year career with the RCMP.

The reputation of the force was also at risk. RCMP relations with the native community were steadily improving. This was no time for a setback. Len Olfert knew he had the advantage of the Christmas Day and Boxing Day holidays which would buy him some time and hold off prying phone calls from the media. However that was all the leeway he had.

Sergeant Peter Montague was the officer in charge of RCMP media relations for British Columbia. He agreed with Superintendent Olfert that unless the whole story of the Michell shooting was explained fully and immediately, the reputation of the force would suffer.

Peter Montague began to set up a series of news conferences, which included the release of RCMP videotapes showing the scene the day after the shooting. This was a profound change in RCMP policy, but it was clearly the only way to set the record straight and justify the need for the pursuit up the West Pavilion Road and for Al Olsen's actions. By way of contrast, when Randy Monk was shot by Constable Hugh Malone at the Pinchie Reserve, there were only two short articles in the *Prince George Citizen* newspaper. Constable Hugh Malone's name was not mentioned in either one.

Due to the more leisurely pace of the Christmas season, the press conferences were set for the following Thursday, December 30. One hour before the scheduled public conferences, Harry Danyluk and Corporal Fred Pearson of the Lillooet detachment met with 50 of Russell Michell's family, friends and members at the Bridge Band office to review the events of the fatal Christmas Eve pursuit on the West Pavilion Road.

Danyluk and Pearson played the transcripts of the radio conversations between the two police cars, showed the video tape and answered all questions. Harry Danyluk also went to some length to explain the forthcoming two-part RCMP investigation of Al Olsen's role in the shooting. Days later, Danyluk would learn his explanation of the seriousness of the investigation had not been totally accepted by the native leaders.

Shortly after the briefing to the Bridge River Band, RCMP media relations officer Peter Montague held a public press conference in Kamloops. Montague ended his statement to the media by saying, "Sergeant Olsen had absolutely no alternative whatsoever. He acted in the only manner he could."

Then he released the radio transcripts, the video tapes and a press release. Obviously Peter Montague hadn't been fully briefed about Rusty Michell's rifle, since he wrote it up as 30/30 instead of a .303, but that aside, the RCMP's forthright statement to the media confirmed Al Olsen's action as self-defence. (Appendix C)

It was a well-orchestrated public relations exercise. The BCTV network even sent a reporter and a camera crew to shoot footage at the start of the West Pavilion Road. This report, coupled with Peter Montague's terse statement that Sergeant Olsen had no choice but to shoot in self defence brought to the public a clear message that Al Olsen had acted in the only way he could.

Rusty Michell was well known as a violent man, particularly when he was drinking. Bradley Jack, Rusty Michell's step-brother told the press, "Rusty was a walking time bomb, he had numerous run ins with the law and had quite a record." Bradley concluded by saying, "There's a long history of problems with Rusty, especially when he's drinking."

Christ'l Roshard, editor of the *Bridge River Lillooet News* wrote a powerful editorial. Christ'l is a perceptive woman, with an eager and genuine interest in people. But more importantly, she brings to her writing a good understanding of native issues, particularly the relationships between the RCMP and the aboriginal community.

Christ'l Roshard had grown up in Lillooet. During her high school years she had worked part-time for the *Bridge River Lillooet News*. In the early seventies she left Lillooet to pursue a marriage, which was brief but reasonably happy, and a career. She lived in Scotland for a while, then returned to Canada and lived in Edmonton, working in advertising and a variety of management jobs. In 1989 she came back to Lillooet and in 1990 went to work at the *Bridge River Lillooet News* as a reporter and, later, editor.

Christ'l Roshard didn't pull any punches in her January 5, editorial. It was an intense piece. She wrote:

> *On Christmas Eve, Rusty Michell was shot and killed by an RCMP officer. That was how he died, but that was not why he died. A person who leads a full and happy life does not point a rifle at a police officer. The "why" must*

be traced far back to many days and years of too much alcohol, too much despair, too much anger.

The why behind Rusty's death will haunt us every time we see another human being heading down the same trail. Revolving through our court system, gaining momentum and anger every time the fine is imposed, the driver's licence is pulled, the weekend jail term begins. Every time the order is given to get counseling for substance abuse, anger management, personal relations.

The system is there to help or change or cure people who do not live within the boundaries of society as a whole. But what about those people who cannot live within them, who have tested the waters of our justice system and skipped across them like a flat stone, making lots of splashes and ripples until they finally simply sink and drown."

Christ'l Roshard finished her editorial with a quote from a chief of the Sto:lo Nation who said, "Don't be angry, pray harder. Within our hearts, pray without anger that we may survive."

Nevertheless, there was anger, some of it legitimate outrage, but a lot of it was politically motivated. Al Olsen had known it had to come and it did.

The immediate RCMP response and up-front explanation of the events leading up to the shooting seemed to have staved off any questions in the mind of the general public. It was clear that Al Olsen had acted in self-defence when confronted by an armed and violent Rusty Michell. Rusty's history of assault with a weapon was a matter of record and there was no denying it.

Still, it didn't take long for the Lillooet native community to turn Russell Michell from a "walking time bomb" to a full-fledged martyr and hero.

On Monday, January 3, Saul Terry, Chief of the Bridge River Indian Band and President of the Union of BC Indian Chiefs, called Christ'l Roshard at the *Bridge River News* and told her he was going to demand a Royal Commission inquiry into policing and the justice system as they related to natives. He was convinced Michell's death could have been avoided, a recurring theme that the native community would play for the next year and throughout the coroner's inquest. Chief Terry was adamant, his comments, published in the Jan. 5, 1994 edition of the *Bridge River Lillooet News*, said, "This is another example of a situation that could have been preventable. Better decisions could have been made in terms of the dispute." Terry also questioned the rationale for such a long chase up a dead-end road saying, "If cooler heads had prevailed, the chase could have been called off and the matter followed through at a later time."

Reading this over-simplistic analysis of the pursuit infuriated Al Olsen, but there nothing he could publicly say in his defence. The two-stage RCMP investigation was just beginning, the crown prosecutor's would take more time and it would be months before the coroner's inquest would be called. The tension in Lillooet was growing, for Al Olsen and his family, it would soon become intolerable.

On January 4, local native leaders met to discuss the Michell shooting and their plan of action. There was more, however. The leaders had an added tragedy on their agenda. Around midnight, Christmas Eve, as Russell Michell lay dead in the snow on the West Pavilion Road, nineteen-year-old Lenore Napoleon left a Christmas party in Lillooet and was last seen walking east towards the Bridge of the 23 Camels which spans the Fraser River.

This in itself was strange since Lenore Napoleon, though living in Kamloops at the time, was staying with her parents over the Christmas season and they lived west of town in the Rancherie area. At a few minutes past midnight, Clarence McIvor, who lived just north of the bridge said he heard a woman "crying in anguish" and asking for help. McIvor phoned the RCMP. There was no response, and sixteen minutes later, McIvor and his wife heard a loud splash. He described the sound this way, "It was as though something had fallen into the Fraser River."

An RCMP officer and a SNTP officer were at the scene by 1:00 a.m. at which time McIvor reported having heard another cry, this one downstream from the bridge. Later McIvor said he saw what looked like hand smears on a lower rail of the bridge deck, as if someone had been hanging there.

Lenore Napoleon's disappearance and the tardiness of a police response to McIvor's phone call, coupled with the Michell shooting prompted the native leaders to call for political action.

Following the January 4 meeting, Chief Saul Terry wrote to Solicitor General Herb Gray and BC Attorney General Colin Gabelmann demanding a Royal Commission be put in place to investigate the policing and justice system as they applied to aboriginal people. His letter was also signed by Russell Michell's step-brother Bradley Jack and band council member Leonard Sampson. (Appendix D)

The letter, particularly since the provincial Attorney General Colin Gabelmann was one of the recipients, caused an immediate concern within the ranks of the

RCMP. The Criminal Justice Branch of the Attorney General's ministry would review the results of the two-stage RCMP investigation, then decide whether or not to lay criminal charges against Al Olsen.

The NDP government at that time was generally considered "soft" on native issues.

Chief Saul Terry's letter, his assertion that the shooting was preventable and that Al Olsen had not made a responsible decision, was a troubling political intervention into the investigation.

Two days later, Chief Clarke Smith of the Fraser Valley Samahquam Band added his voice to Saul Terry's with more correspondence. (Appendix E) In the next few weeks, the situation in Lillooet worsened. Al Olsen was receiving threats and Al's wife Joan received a particularly threatening phone call. Joan was home alone, when the phone rang, she picked it up and the male voice said, "You fucking bitch, we're going to get you, your husband's an Indian killer."

That what the last straw and at the end of January, Al Olsen announced he was leaving Lillooet. His opening statement to the press was understandably terse. He said, "My family does not need the stress and hassle. My family and I have enjoyed living here. This is an excellent community. However, to be effective in continuing to improve relations in the community I needed the trust and assistance of everyone. Regretfully, since the events of Christmas Eve, this support has been withdrawn by the aboriginal leadership." Then, in a more conciliatory manner, and in an acknowledgment of the difficulty the native leaders were having, he said, "I understand the reasons behind the move — however this has made my position as detachment commander ineffective. For the sake of the community and my family, I have decided to leave."

He made a closing reference to the way the RCMP had improved its understanding of the native community, little knowing his words would be echoed by a respected native elder, some ten months later.

"I can only hope, with the arrival of a new detachment commander, that this will allow the community as a whole to move forward. I do not believe anyone wishes to go back to the relationships of the early 1990s."

In 1990, there was a lot of anger in the native community which had resulted in a series of native road blocks on the Duffy Lake Road, the BC Rail line and on a highway right-of-way that went through the Fountain Reserve outside of Lillooet.

Al Olsen stayed in Lillooet until June so his two boys could finish the school year. Then he was transferred to the Kamloops RCMP Subdivision where he spent the next 13 months with the commercial crime unit.

But the ill feelings didn't go away with the announcement of Al Olsen's transfer. The Lillooet native community continued to question the events on the West Pavilion Road and even STNP Constable Keith McKay received two threatening phone calls. Although a native and essentially an innocent bystander to Michell's death, McKay was worried enough about the threats that for the four months following the Michell shooting, he carried his .38 Police Special Smith & Wesson revolver with him at all times.

On February 21, Attorney General Colin Gabelmann sent his response to Chief Saul Terry. (Appendix F) Al Olsen wasn't aware of the letter, but he knew by now that the two- part internal RCMP investigation had cleared him of any criminal actions and the results of that investigation was being reviewed by Kamloops Crown Counsel Hermann Rohrmoser. Al Olsen felt certain that Rohrmoser would recommend that no criminal charges be laid against him. However, there was no telling what might happen when the report was received by the more politically-motivated officials in Victoria.

In December 1993, Aboriginal Affairs Minister John Cashore had introduced the Treaty Negotiation Commission in an attempt to settle the growing number of outstanding native land claims. The treaty process required all British Columbian native bands to buy into the negotiations. The NDP government desperately needed the native community on side for the treaty commission to be a success.

Adding to Olsen's concern was the knowledge that the Attorney General of the day, Colin Gabelmann, was a career politician, not a lawyer. He seemed to have no concept of the neutrality and objectivity of the justice system. Plus, it was widely assumed that Gabelmann was easily influenced by special interest groups and was "soft" on law and order issues. Many people felt he was susceptible to political pressure from the aboriginal community, particularly with Saul Terry pushing for a Royal Commission into RCMP relations with the natives.

Troubling too were rumors around Kamloops suggesting that although Rohrmoser's report, submitted to Victoria on April 13, had recommended no charges be laid, but there were forces at work in the Attorney General's ministry recommending that Olsen face criminal charges.

It was a gut-wrenching time for Al Olsen; the weeks dragged on with no news. Finally, Regional Crown Counsel Hermann Rohrmoser called a press conference to be held at the Lillooet Government Agent's office on Monday May 4.

Christ'l Roshard of the *Bridge River News* was there along with reporters and a TV news crew from Kamloops. Attending Rohrmoser's press conference were Chief Saul Terry, several members of Michell's family and three RCMP officers including Superintendent Len Olfert. Al Olsen did not attend, although he was still the senior officer in charge of the Lillooet Detachment.

Rohrmoser had a prepared press release. (Appendix G) He read a prepared statement, saying, "This opinion is based on a consideration of all the evidence, which included a complaint that Mr. Michell had his children with him in the vehicle, was prohibited from driving and possessing a firearm and yet was reportedly driving while impaired and in possession of a firearm."

Hermann Rohrmoser continued with a description of the pursuit, the collision between Al Olsen's police car and the green Oldsmobile, then concluded with this recount of the final minutes: "Sergeant Olsen was still seated in the driver's seat of the police car when Mr. Michell approached the driver's side window, now pointing a rifle at Sergeant Olsen at close range. Sergeant Olsen, believing he would be shot, fired several rounds of his service revolver through the closed driver's side window. "Rohrmoser's last sentence wasn't needed but he had to end the incident, calmly he finished his statement saying, "Mr. Michell died at the scene."

None of this satisfied Chief Saul Terry who seemed to never miss an opportunity to play to the media, particularly when TV cameras were running. Stepping to the front, Terry continued to press for a Royal Commission, he said, "We demand a full and public inquiry. Police and

Indian relations were not good, not only here in Lillooet but across the province." Terry added, "I don't make this request lightly."

Saul Terry went on to say that the Bridge River Band had hired their own investigators, Jim Malone and Gerry Oleman, to provide the band with what ever additional information they could find about Rusty Michell's death prior to the coroner's inquest. As it later turned out, neither Malone nor Oleman were unable to provide any evidence to further the band's investigation.

Regional Coroner Bob Graham also attended the Lillooet press conference. He announced that a coroner's inquest with a local jury, was scheduled for June 22. Graham was well aware of the lingering hostility towards Al Olsen and he took the time to stress that the coroner's inquest was not a criminal investigation. "That has already been done," he said.

When advised of the inquest date, Al Olsen felt some apprehension, but also a sense of relief. He vividly remembered the Randy Monk inquest at the Tachie Reserve and how it had torn his emotions. The Russell Michell inquest would be easier to handle. Unlike Randy Monk, Michell had a long record of violence and armed assault. No shooting can ever be justified, but there was no doubt that last Christmas Eve, Russell Michell was looking for trouble.

Al Olsen also knew that the coroner's inquest would thankfully and officially put an end to the Michell shooting. After five months of waiting in what seemed like a bureaucratic never-never land, Al Olsen would have his day in court. He would finally have the opportunity to speak his mind, to describe the violent incident and to publicly face his accusers. And, perhaps as at the Randy

Monk inquest, some healing just might take place. That would be good, Olsen thought.

There was little healing taking place on the Bridge River Reserve, though, after Hermann Rohrmoser's announcement that charges against Olsen would not be laid. Chief Saul Terry still wanted to use the Michell shooting as an example of a how the justice system had failed the native population. To this end he sought funding from the coroner's office to help the Band prepare for the inquest.

In British Columbia, there is no provision for such funding and Coroner Bob Graham had to advise Saul Terry that although the Bridge River Band would have official status at the inquest, his office had no provision to provide them with funding. Never one to give up, Saul Terry next asked for a postponement and on June 20, two days before the inquest was to begin, he got one. He then issued a brief statement (Appendix H).

Coroner Bob Graham later said the Russell Michell inquest would be put off until October. Although he could not provide funding assistance to the Bridge River Band, he hoped the delay would give them the time to raise what ever money they needed.

This was not what Al Olsen wanted to hear. What should have been a straight-forward, and final step in the Michell shooting was becoming a political football, with the RCMP taking most of the kicking.

Although he could not provide funding, Bob Graham then announced the inquest would begin Tuesday, October 25. Graham thought the final four days of the week would give ample time to conclude the inquest.

But again there was another delay. In the ensuing months, Coroner Graham had compiled a lengthy witness list and was concerned that a four-day inquest would not provide enough time for all witnesses to be heard. He moved the inquest to December 12, although it turned out his fears were unjustified. Joan Olsen heard about this date change on the radio even before Al was notified. With the newest delay Al Olsen was beginning to wonder if this ordeal was ever going to end.

13

AT LONG LAST, after two delays and almost a year since the 1993 Christmas Eve shooting, the coroner's office held its official inquest into Russell Michell's death.

The inquest began at 10:00 a.m. December 12, 1994. In order to give the native community a feeling of connection to the proceedings, and avoid any feelings of discrimination or alienation, Regional Coroner Bob Graham arranged to use the Lillooet Native Friendship Centre for the Russell Michell inquest. The Friendship Centre is a spacious building with open log beams forming the roof structure. It has a seating area which can accommodate up to 100 people; about thirty were in attendance that morning. There was a skiff of snow on the ground and the weather conditions were similar to what they had been fifty weeks earlier on Christmas Eve, 1993.

Coroner Bob Graham sat at table at the front of the room. Those attending sat in rows facing Bob Graham. To Graham's left, the five jury members sat at a similar table, their backs to the wall, at a right angle to the Graham's table.

Selected as jury foreman was Dave Horne, an employee of the BC Ministry of Forests. The other four members were Carey McDonald, a social worker; Ida Foisy, an employee of the Lillooet School District; Yvonne LaRochelle and Victor Adrian. Yvonne LaRochelle was a native, and a civilian employee of the tribal STNP. Victor Adrian was also a native Indian. Adrian lived in Lillooet and worked for Ainsworth Lumber. His father, Victor Adrian Sr. was a past Chief of the Fountain Indian Band. All the jury members were long-time residents of Lillooet.

A court reporter with two tape machines sat at another table, just to the right of Bob Graham and facing the rows of seats. Witnesses would be called to a stand to the right of the court reporter's table, while lawyers acting for the various witnesses would pose their questions from a stand on Bob Graham's left, in front of the jury.

Bob Graham was ideally suited to the job. He brought a solid founding in the criminal justice system and an empathetic understanding to the office of Coroner. Graham had started his career as a municipal police officer in Nelson BC. He then worked for the provincial Sheriff's office, moved next to Court Services and became the Regional Coroner for the Kamloops area in the mid 1980s.

That day, he was dressed conservatively in a grey suit, shirt and tie, but had chosen a pair of bright red socks decorated with prancing white reindeer to make his own Christmas-season fashion statement

Graham opened the inquest. He spoke softly, yet with determination. He was well aware of the underlying racial tensions. He began with the following introduction.

"A coroner's inquest in the province of British Columbia is a public inquiry designed to serve three primary functions. First, it is a means for public ascertainment of fact related to death: specifically, who the deceased was, how the deceased came to his death, when the deceased came to his death, where the deceased came to his death and by what means he died."

Bob Graham spoke slowly. He was aware of the hostility that had festered in the native community following Rusty Michell's death and he wanted to make it perfectly clear that a coroner's inquest was not a court case, nor was the RCMP, or Al Olsen on trial. He was aware, though, that there was some expectation particularly from the Bridge River Band who had hired legal counsel to represent it at the inquest.

Many Bridge River natives were still convinced that had the RCMP pursuit of Russell Michell been called off, he would still be alive today. From that premise, many band members concluded that Al Olsen had deliberately set out to shoot Russell Michell.

Bob Graham continued with his explanation of what was to come: "Secondly, a coroner's inquest is a means of determining if the death was preventable, and if so, to make recommendations, and that will be the responsibility of the jury to do so, recommendations that will prevent future loss of life under similar circumstances."

Members of the RCMP, who attended the inquest sat quietly as Bob Graham continued. But it wasn't lost on any of the Mounties that in similar circumstances, when a drunk and violent man with a record of weapon assaults points a high powered rifle at an armed policeman, a loss of life would probably be the result.

Coroner Bob Graham went on with his comments: "Thirdly, a coroner's inquest is the means of satisfying the community that no circumstances surrounding the death of one its members, will be overlooked, concealed or ignored."

Graham then advised the jury: "I would caution the members of the jury to disregard anything that you may have heard or read prior to this inquest, with reference to the death. You must base your verdict and recommendations, if any, solely on the evidence you will hear at this inquest."

Coroner Graham's next comments were of little comfort to many Bridge River Band members, who still saw the inquest as a high-profile way to make a political point. Whether Bob Graham was aware of this or not was not known. Nevertheless, he was absolutely clear on the purpose of a coroner's inquest.

"The inquest is a fact-finding body." Graham paused, then stressed the next sentence before continuing. "It is not a fault-finding body. You are not to judge the guilt or innocence of anyone . . . no one is on trial. Evidence will be given by duly summoned witnesses and also by witnesses who have been called by those designated to stand. If any other person wishes to give relevant evidence pertaining to this death, such evidence may be heard later in the hearing.

"The strict rules of evidence do not apply to a coroner's inquest, as no one is on trial. Since all of the witnesses who have been duly summoned to the coroner's inquest are obligated to answer the questions put to them, and as such answers may tend to incriminate them, the witnesses are entitled to ask for, and receive the protection of various evidence acts and the Charter of Rights in Canada. Their answers then shall not be proceedable against them in future court proceedings, unless the witness has committed perjury."

Bob Graham ended his introductory explanation of the coroner's inquest process by carefully explaining how witnesses would be called and questioned. He then gave a neutral and brief description of the events leading up to and including Russell's death.

The first witness called was Kathy James. She was sworn in. Counsel for the Coroner's office Fred Kaatz put the first questions to Kathy.

Carefully and deliberately, Kaatz reviewed the background details beginning with Kathy's common-law relationship Michell. He asked about the children they had and the years they'd lived together.

Kaatz then led Kathy through the sequence of events that Christmas Eve — Rusty's arrival, his obvious drunkenness.

When Kaatz asked Kathy what brought on the call to the RCMP, Kathy answered slowly, pausing as she spoke about her terror that evening. "When he came home . . . he was very intoxicated, he was getting mad . . . and angry . . . he scared me!"

Kaatz's next set of questions gradually expanded on the desperate scene that evening: "When you say . . . he got mad and angry, what did he do? Was he . . . was he . . . violent at all . . . in any way?

Kathy hesitated, thought for a moment, the scene becoming vivid in her mind, then she slowly answered: "Um . . . yeah he was throwing the table around and he smashed the glass on the oven door . . . and he was hollering, like . . . he was mad."

Kaatz continued his questioning of Kathy James. Her quiet yet disturbing answers hung in the air. Kaatz asked about the ages of Kathy's children.

She responded, "Eleven, two are aged eight — one of them was premature. Then there's a seven-year-old and a five-year-old." Native and non-native alike understood the terror she must felt that evening. They'd seen and heard it all before. As Kathy spoke, it was easy to visualize her children cowering as Rusty Michell went out of control yelling, throwing plates and smashing furniture. As she answered, Kathy James painted an ugly and disturbing picture of a violently abusive situation.

Under further questioning, Kathy described her terrified phone call to the RCMP, her concern that Russell may have taken one or more of the children and that she had been able to confirm that Russell had taken a rifle and some shells.

Fred Kaatz had set the scene well, as James confirmed beyond any doubt that she had every good reason to be concerned for her safety and that of her children that evening.

Al Olsen's lawyer, Jim Jardine, was next to question Kathy James. His questions were brief, since Fred Kaatz had already substantially established that Kathy was convinced she desperately needed police protection that evening.

Applying the first rule of questioning — that is only asking questions to which the answers are known — Jim Jardine reinforced the fear that Kathy had felt that evening when she called the police.

He began by focusing on Rusty's record of spousal assault. He asked Kathy about her written statement to the police and posed this question: "Now as I understand it, the reason that you were scared this particular evening was because there had been previous incidents where you had been assaulted by Rusty."

Kathy took a moment to answer, then softly replied, "Yes."

Jim Jardine continued. "Yeah . . . but . . . in relation to that, he had . . . he'd punched you and slapped you and bruised you up and left you with some black eyes in the past."

Again a pause, the room was still, then the quiet answer, "Yes."

Jardine pressed on with this line of questioning. It was critical to show that the RCMP had acted out of a genuine concern for Kathy and the children's well-being.

"And is it also correct that on this particular night, the first thing which set him off was . . . was that one of your boys was feeding the dog?" Jim Jardine was establishing a disturbing pattern of violent behavior.

Kathy seemed intrigued by the question, and for the first time during her time on the witness stand she began to explain Rusty's actions. "I'm not too sure if that's what set him off, but he was coming up the back stairs and my son was feeding the dog and he got mad at him . . . I don't know why."

"And that was your son Kevin, right?"

"Yes."

By this point, Jardine had clearly established Kathy James's fear and her need for help. He next asked questions about Rusty throwing dishes at Kathy.

"Did he . . . did he throw the plate . . . uh . . . his supper at you . . . uh . . . when you were in the kitchen?"

"As I was walking out."

Jim Jardine pressed on, he needed Kathy's description of Russell's violent behavior on the record.

"And then after that you went back into the kitchen where he threw the plate at you and it hit the cupboard above your head?"

Kathy was seeing it all over again. With disturbing candor, she corrected Jardine's question, "No, above the fridge," she replied. Even after a year the frightening events were still vivid in her mind.

"And then after that you went back into the kitchen and you became concerned about your safety and that's when you ran over to Mary Peters' house, is that right?"

"Yes."

"Now the rest of your involvement in this matter was by you trying to communicate to the police on the telephone?"

"Yes."

"Thank you Mr. Coroner, those are my questions."

The next lawyer to question Kathy was Renee Taylor, one of the two lawyers appearing for the Bridge River Indian Band. Taylor attempted to soften the abusive side of Russell Michell. "Now you have said in evidence today that you were afraid of Russell. Did you think that he would be beating you that night?"

Kathy's answer was quiet, but confident. She said, "No."

Taylor continued. "And how long had it been since he had last beaten you or abused you physically?"

"About two years."

"And did you think that he would harm the children that night physically?"

"No."

"Did he ever hit the children . . . in anger?"

Kathy paused. This was clearly a difficult question; she looked as if she was ready to answer, but her eyes rimmed with tears. Finally she spoke. "No."

By now she was sobbing, unable to continue. Renee Taylor could see Kathy needed some time.

"Could I see if the witness needs a moment, Mr. Coroner."

Then in a reassuring way she said to Kathy, "Kathy just you tell me when you feel OK to answer questions or we can stop for a while."

Kathy sat quietly for a few minutes, then she looked at Renee Taylor, nodded her head to show she could carry on.

Taylor continued with her questions. "When you phoned the police that night, what did you want them to do?"

Kathy's response was refreshingly candid. "I wanted somebody to come and help me and just keep Russell away from me."

That didn't seem to be the answer Taylor wanted. "So you wanted Russell arrested that night?"

There was a long pause, Kathy didn't answer.

Renee Taylor continued, attempting again to establish Rusty Michell's nonviolent side.

"When you were asked by the dispatcher whether or not Russell had a weapon did you ever think Russell would use that weapon that evening."

"No."

"Did you give any thought to why he may have had the gun?"

"No."

Renee Taylor switched the topic. "When did you find out . . . and how did you find out Russell had been shot?"

Kathy didn't answer.

"Did you phone the detachment to ask where Russell was any time over the evening?"

"Yes several times."

"And what did they say to you?"

"They just told me to wait . . . 'til somebody comes to . . . ."

Taylor filled in the answer, "To talk to you. And did they say why they were going to send somebody to talk to you?"

"No." Kathy was still visibly upset and her soft voice was shaking. She remembered how stressful the early Christmas morning had been.

"So how did you find out Russell had been shot?"

"There were friends of mine who heard it on the scanner."

"OK."

Again, Kathy broke down crying.

Taylor asked if a member of the Victim's Services could assist Kathy. When Kathy was ready to testify again, Taylor, by using the emotion Kathy felt that morning, attempted to portray the RCMP as uncaring.

"So do you know what time you were told by your friends that the scanner had reported a shooting?"

"I figured about ten or ten thirty in the evening."

"And did your friends tell you they thought it was Rusty?"

"They told me it was him." Kathy was still crying.

"Your friends . . . they heard his name on the scanner?"

"Yes."

"And when you . . . you continued to try and call the police department to find out what had happened?"

"Yes."

"And what were you told?"

"They told me that no one . . . they didn't know anything . . . there was nobody around to talk. They were out."

"How did you finally determine yourself that this in fact had happened . . that Russell had been shot?"

"How did I find out?"

"Yes. Did you ever go to the police station?"

Kathy next described her trip up the West Pavilion Road. "Before we went to the police station . . . there were four of us . . we went out to the West Pavilion to find out what had happened."

"Out to the road where the shooting had occurred?"

"Yes . . . and we got part way up there and everyone was coming down and . ." Kathy paused for a moment, her mind back on the West Pavilion Road. She remembered the convoy of police cars, the cold morning air — it was always colder just before dawn. She hadn't realized at the time but she knew now that Russell's body must have been in one of the cars.

Slowly she continued, tears in her eyes, "And they told us to wait, back in town . . . at the police station."

"Who was they, who was it that you spoke to?"

Kathy was still sobbing; these were disturbing details to remember.

"I don't know who it was, I didn't talk to them, it was somebody else."

"Was it the police, or an ambulance attendant?"

"It was the police."

"And so did you go back to the police station?"

"Yes."

"And is that when you were told?"

"Yes."

"And do you know what time that was?"

"It must have been about six or six thirty in the morning."

"So about . . . approximately eight hours later after you had first hand it on the scanner you were officially notified that he had been shot."

"Yes."

At this point Renee Taylor changed her line of questioning. She wanted to use Kathy's testimony to soften Rusty's record. "Did Russell get into fights in the bars as far as you knew?"

Kathy was quiet for a moment then replied, "No."

"And there is one reference in one of the statements given . . . did Russell ever hit you with an ashtray?"

"Not that I can recall."

"When Russell left your house that night, what did you think he would do, where did you think he was going?"

"I didn't know."

"You didn't think about it?"

"No."

"Were you afraid he would come back and hurt you that night?

Kathy couldn't forget the terror she'd felt that evening. Her response was slow in coming, but even a year later she couldn't deny the terrible fear she'd felt for her family and herself. Slowly she answered, "Yes."

"And so you wanted the police to help you."

At this point Taylor turned the question on Kathy, not imlying guilt but attempting to paint a harsh picture of the RCMP.

"Did it ever occur to you that Russell might be shot?

"No."

Taylor's next question, posed a cruel and difficult assumption. "Would you have called the police . . . if you thought that Russell would have been shot?"

Kathy was quiet for a moment, then she quietly answered, "No."

"I have no further questions, Mr. Coroner."

Bonnie Michell, Russell Michell's younger sister was next to testify. Under questioning from Fred Kaatz, Bonnie Michell admitted that Russell had a violent side when he was drinking.

Al Olsen's counsel, Jim Jardine had no questions for Bonnie Michell. Renee Taylor then sought the floor and asked a series of questions, dealing mostly with Russell's inability to handle alcohol. Her last question to Bonnie Michell attempted again to soften Russell's violent nature.

She asked, "Do you believe he was capable of harming anyone . . . with a gun?"

Bonnie Michell answered quickly, "No."

Following Bonnie Michell's testimony, the audio tape of the radio transmissions between Kamloops Telecoms, Kathy James and both police cars was played for the coroner's inquest. It was a moving experience. As the voices filled the large Friendship Centre meeting room, there was no hiding Kathy's fright when she first called the RCMP — her terror was real. As the taped conversations played out the pursuit, it was also clear that Stan Walstrom and Al Olsen had experienced their share of terrifying moments that evening.

Stan Walstrom's nervousness came through on more than a few occasions on the tape. It was readily apparent that from the beginning of the pursuit, Walstrom had expected serious trouble from Michell.

Al Olson's voice was recorded from the time he left his home driveway in Lillooet. He remained cool throughout the evening, only showing extreme emotion when he described the fatal confrontation with Rusty Michell.

Constable Stan Walstrom was called next to testify. As he was sworn in, it was interesting for those who didn't know the young officer to put a face to the distinctive excited voice they'd heard two hours earlier on the RCMP communications tape. Walstrom's questioning began with Fred Kaatz, who quickly but methodically led Stan Walstrom through the events leading up to the pursuit. First, Kaatz had Walstrom describe how during his time as a new member of the RCMP in Lillooet, he had become familiar with Michell's long and violent police record. Then Kaatz led Walstrom to the first call he had received from Kamloops Telecoms, advising him of Kathy James's frantic phone call and the damage Michell was doing to her house.

Next, Kaatz confirmed Walstrom's call to STNP Corporal Keith McKay for backup. Kaatz was also quick to have Stan Walstrom state for the record that he was a status Indian from the Stellako Band, part of the Carrier/ Sekani Tribal Council. With McKay's and Walstrom's native background soundly established, to everyone one in the room it was clear that counsel for the Bridge River Band could put aside any accusations of a racially motivated police over-reaction to the troubling events happening of Christmas Eve a year ago.

Fred Kaatz had no more questions.

Al Olsen's counsel, Jim Jardine, was next. Jardine wanted to get to the police radio jargon, just in case audio tape played earlier had left any doubt why the pursuit had taken place. Referring to the transcript of the communications tape, Jardine asked Stan Walstrom, "What's a forty-three-er?"

Stan Walstrom eagerly answered. "A forty-three-er in police jargon is referring to person who is intoxicated and that's under the Liquor Control Licensing Act . . . uh . . . the number of a section under that Control Licensing Act which indicates an authority to arrest someone for being drunk."

Walstrom, appearing nervous, went on explaining the police radio shorthand. "It's common jargon used on the airwaves . . . uh radio waves . . . between Telecoms and police officers."

The explanation was more than Jim Jardine needed but it had served his purpose. Jardine responded, "Uh . . . OK because at page three of the Telecoms transmission . . . uh . . . you receive a message from the Telecoms operator to the effect that he's forty-three . . . started trashing the house, so that meant he's intoxicated . . . is that right?"

"That's right, it was basic jargon indicating he was intoxicated, or drunk."

Jardine carried on. It was essential to show the police had acted quickly to Kathy's frightened phone call. "Now you had a conversation with Kathy James on the telephone, is that right?"

"Yes sir."

"And what did you hear in relation to the children in that telephone conversation?"

Stan Walstrom checked his notes, since the question required an extensive explanation. The answer was a little longer than Jim Jardine had anticipated, but it made the point.

"She . . . uh . . . she didn't mention anything about the children at that time, she just mentioned that Rusty was

. . . uh . . . he was drunk and that he had trashed the place and that she wanted us to come out there. And . . . uh . . . it was subsequent to that, that I learned about the children being taken by . . . Mr. Michell and that these children were possibly being taken up to Bonnie Michell's place."

Jim Jardine stayed with a line of questioning that not only supported the RCMP response but also underscored Kathy James's concern for the safety of her self and her children. "And at the time that you spoke with her would you describe for us what her emotions were like?"

Stan Walstrom thought for a moment then quietly answered: "Well . . . like I said, Ms. James was very emotional, very distraught, very upset, I guess . . . fearful."

Jardine then asked Stan Walstrom about briefing Al Olsen over the police car radios on Rusty Michell's state of intoxication. Walstrom's responses were straightforward, echoing what the inquest had heard earlier from the RCMP audio tape.

Next Jardine focused on Michell's rifle and when Stan Walstrom had visually confirmed that Michell was armed.

"Uh . . . there's one other portion where during the course of the time, you observed him reaching to his right. Could you describe the motion you that you were able to observe of Mr. Michell as he was driving the vehicle, what he was doing, when he appeared to be reaching to his right?"

Stan Walstrom took a minute to put his thoughts together and then described Rusty Michell's erratic driving. "Well . . . Mr. Michell's vehicle speed had dropped dramatically. We had been basically travelling in the 50 to 60 kilometre range consistently for some time . . . and at around the 40 . . . uh . . . 42 kilometre mark, Mr. Michell's vehicle slowed down to below 20 kilometers an hour. At this time Mr. Michell took both of his hands off the steering wheel and was leaning completely to his extreme right . . . where we could barely see the top of his head. We could see he was reaching far over to his right, and then he sat upright again and that's when we first observed the rifle."

Jim Jardine wanted every reference to Michell's rifle on the inquest record. He pressed Stan Walstrom for more details. "And at that portion just before 20:44 hours . . . 8:44 p.m. where then you say, The rifle is sitting upright Kamloops, copy that, it's sitting upright. Did you see him reaching at any other time that you can recall?"

"Well yes," Stan replied. "At several times during the pursuit, Mr. Michell had slowed his vehicle down to 20 . . . 30 kilometers an hour and at these times he was moving his hands down around by his right side . . . and . . . uh he appeared to be fiddling with the gun and . . . uh . . . we couldn't see exactly what he was doing but he was definitely trying to do something with the gun . . . that's all we could see."

Jim Jardine didn't need much more than that. He had clearly established that Rusty Michell was armed and was obviously trying to load the rifle while driving his car.

Stan Walstrom was questioned next by Susie Gray, assistant counsel for the Bridge River Band. Gray had an energetic style of questioning, although at times she appeared unprepared and had trouble distinguishing between the various ranks of the RCMP.

She began by questioning Stan Walstrom about his knowledge of the area. "Sergeant Walstrom, you said you'd been working in the Lillooet area for three and a half years, is that correct?"

Constable Stan Walstrom was taken a bit by the sudden promotion, but for the meantime kept his answers simple. He replied, "That's . . . that's close. Yes."

Gray continued, "So I take it from that . . . that you're quite familiar with the area and . . . uh . . . and well including the Reserve area and . . . the area that this chase took place in?"

Walstrom took a minute following this question to expand on his limited knowledge of the West Pavilion Road. "Well somewhat, I mean I've been out to the area maybe six times . . . I'd never been as far as far as the chase was . . . I'd never been past the 50 kilometre . . . but I knew there were residences going up there."

Susie Gray pressed Walstrom for more details. "What did you know of the West Pavilion Road? Had you been told it went any certain distance? What did you know of it? I realize you hadn't been the full distance."

Stan Walstrom's answer wasn't all that informative. "Basically, I knew there was the Big Bar ferry out in the area and I'd never been as far as the Big Bar ferry . . . ."

As Walstrom thought more about the question, Gray interjected, "And how far would that be from Lillooet?

"My initial understanding, I thought it was about 120 kilometres."

At this point, Gray had Walstrom confirm that last Christmas Eve the road ended at the Fraser River.

"And the Big Bar ferry, is that a ferry that runs year round in your knowledge?"

"Uh . . . no it can't run all year round because when the Fraser freezes up . . . well it's a water-run ferry, I believe . . . and it can't run in winter."

At this point, Gray returned to the transcript of the radio communications and summarily went through the sequence of events from the start of the police pursuit at the beginning of West Pavilion Road: Stan Walstrom spotting the green Oldsmobile and his decision to follow and apprehend; then the visual confirmation of Michell as his car skidded sideways; Walstrom's acknowledgment that the roads were icy; the rifle sighting; and the call from Kamloops Telecoms that Kathy had the children.

Susie Gray continued with this set of questions:

"So at this point . . . I take it . . . it looks like you're about 33 kilometres up the road . . . and so what you can confirm at that point, if you can just agree, or disagree, is that you know who's driving the vehicle . . . Rusty Michell . . . you know that he's prohibited from driving . . . uh . . . it's believed he's impaired, it's confirmed that there are no kids in the car . . . would you agree that all those things are confirmed at that time?"

Stan Walstrom knew where this line of questioning was going, he quietly answered, "That's correct."

Susie Gray had Stan Walstrom hung out on a dead-end line of questioning.

"And I guess you can also confirm that he's heading up a road which you believe to go approximately 100 to 120 kilometres to a dead end?"

"That's right."

"Did you discuss at this time whether you should call off the chase . . . with Sergeant Olsen?"

With this question Gray returned to Chief Saul Terry's first argument, which lead to the simple conclusion that calling off the pursuit would have been the better solution.

Walstrom stressed the seriousness of the situation. "We discussed it and we were concerned that . . . Mr. Michell may have a loaded gun and we didn't know what his actions were and what he was going to do if he possibly returned to Lillooet from there. He was basically unpredictable . . . and that was one of our main concerns."

Susie Gray quickly interrupted at this point. Raising her voice and quickening the pace, she pounced on the next question, asking, "Constable Walstrom, how could he have returned to Lillooet, other than by the road you were on? Was there any other way he could get back to Lillooet?"

"Not that I'm aware of." Walstrom replied.

Susie Gray had made her point; in her mind this was a gotcha. "OK" she said.

Stan Walstrom couldn't let her get away with reaching such a speedy conclusion. Quickly he added, "But if we let him go we would have no way of knowing what his actions would be."

Gray stuck with her question, "But . . . what I'm trying to get at though is . . . the only way he could return . . . physically return to Lillooet was along on the same road that you were on . . . OK?

Stan Walstrom confirmed the obvious, "To my knowledge that's correct."

With the dead-end road concept firmly in place, Susie Gray turned to the question of a roadblock. "Did you discuss at this point the possibility of setting up a road block?"

Stan Walstrom repeated what Al Olsen had first said to that suggestion. "Yes we had discussed that and . . . uh . . . Sergeant Olsen indicated that we didn't want to be basically sitting around if he decided to find us. In other words, if we had set up a road block we were concerned that we might be sitting targets. As we'd seen the rifle, and had confirmed that the rifle was in the vehicle by Mrs. James and so our concern was that we didn't want to be injured."

This response didn't satisfy Ms. Gray. "Well my understanding would be that if you set up a roadblock . . . you can correct me . . . I take it setting up a road block would mean that you would stop the car in a certain location and block the road. In other words block him from returning back . . past you and back into Lillooet. That's my understanding of a road block."

Stan Walstrom remained polite and informative, although it wasn't lost on anyone who knew the West Pavilion Road in winter, what Gray was suggesting bordered on the suicidal. "Yes, that's basically how a road block would work. However, if we did do this, we're highly visible from the road and the vehicle is highly visible . . . which may have led us to be seen by Mr. Michell and he could have departed his vehicle at the time . . . and we didn't want to be sitting there . . . and possibly be targets."

Susie Gray didn't seem to understand that Russell Michell had a considerable firepower advantage over the RCMP officers. "But if in fact you continued the chase and did eventually convince him to stop, what would the difference in that situation, than one in which you had stopped and set up a road block?"

Stan Walstrom thought for a moment, cleared his throat and slowly replied, "Basically, our concern was to try and predict what Mr. Michell was going to do, that's why we kept pursuing him at the time . . . we didn't want him to . . . we didn't want him to get out of the vehicle before we had the opportunity to get close enough to him . . . with him having the rifle and having a chance to shoot at us."

Gray seemed to accept Stan Walstrom's concern about Michell's rifle and superior firepower. She continued, "Now with respect to him getting out of the vehicle actually you did discuss that . . . and I believe when you discussed that with Sergeant Olsen he advised you that if in fact Rusty exited the vehicle . . . on foot that you were not to follow him. Is that correct?"

Stan Walstrom had no problems with that question, those had been Olsen's orders, "That is correct," he quickly replied.

"And if he did that, than you were supposed to turn around and get out of there."

Stan Walstrom replied slowly and deliberately; he had to make her understand they were in serious danger of being shot that evening.

"Basically . . . get out of there as soon as you can, because he had the rifle and we had to get out of there before he had a chance to shoot."

Following that answer, Susie Gray finally seemed to understand that the officers were a genuinely concerned for their lives and, that on the night of that long Christmas Eve pursuit, they had no reason to doubt that Rusty Michell had every intent of shooting to kill. Gray changed the subject and questioned Stan Walstrom about his radio transmissions and the updating of his position and the road conditions.

Walstrom politely and carefully explained RCMP policy, which is to continually update the Telecoms centre on your location and always advise members following you about road conditions, especially when they were hazardous to driving.

Susie Gray next questioned Stan Walstrom on RCMP procedures during a hazardous pursuit. She had a copy of the hazardous pursuit policy in her hand and asked: "Now . . . with respect to the RCMP procedures on pursuits . . . would you refer to the operations procedures policy? What

I have here is the actual policy, would you actually refer to these things?" I mean somehow you'd be advised of the procedures and policies."

Stan Walstrom found the question exasperating, and to some extent belittling, but he responded in his own polite way. "That is correct . . . as a junior officer coming out of training, you go through a process called the field recruit program. It's on-the-job training and it's part of your job to go over operations manuals and then you're actually tested on your knowledge of the policies."

Susie Gray, still confused about RCMP ranks then asked Walstrom whether he could have unilaterally called off the pursuit. "Sergeant Walstrom, you were in a position as one of the drivers of one the vehicles to actually call off the chase on your own, isn't that correct?"

Stan Walstrom disagreed with this, replying, "Well, I felt obligated to ensure that Michell was apprehended."

Gray broke in. She wanted to pursue her own line of questioning. "Well I appreciate that, but you could have made that decision . . to call off the chase."

Walstrom disagreed again. "No, I would have actually have had to have the advice of an acting NCO . . . a non-commissioned officer to make that decision."

Gray wouldn't let go of this line of questioning. She hung on, asking, "But it's within your authority to make that decision, isn't that right?"

Stan Walstrom seemed pained by the question as he said, "Well basically that authority is given to the superior officer . . . the Sergeant or the Corporal . . . and if they were to give the instruction to call off the pursuit . . . then that would end it."

Susie Gray continued, this time quoting RCMP policy. "Well according to the operations manual it says, the decision to abandon a pursuit may be made by the driver of a police pursuit vehicle, isn't that correct?"

Stan Walstrom looked at her, it was clear he found this line of questioning tedious. Slowly he answered, "Yes."

Gray continued, reading from the RCMP hazardous pursuit manual, "Or the senior member directly involved, or a supervisor monitoring the progress. So you're one of those people who could have made that decision."

This time Stan Walstrom answered quickly, "Yes, but I felt obligated that . . . we try and arrest Mr. Michell."

Susie Gray raised her voice, she figured she had Walstrom in a corner of his own making, "But if Mr. Michell had continued on the route . . . and you had returned to Lillooet . . . could you not have located him the following day and arrested him then? I suppose that's hypothetical but . . . ."

Walstrom broke in saying, "That 's possible but like I said before we didn't know . . . uh, he was unpredictable . . . he'd already been involved in some sort of a violent incident and we just wanted to make sure that we contain him as soon as possible."

Susie Gray leapt in, stating, "But again . . you have testified that he was on a road that went some 100, 120 kilometres to a dead end."

Quickly she referred to the operations manual "I'm referring to the section that says, "Before initiating or continuing a hazardous pursuit, consider the following; and then it says, in section one, If the subject is known or can be identified and," Gray paused, she stressed the next point, " And . . whether or not apprehension can be affected at some later time." (Appendix I)

Gray stopped to let that regulation sink in. Then she continued, saying, "Now you knew who Rusty Michell was and you certainly knew where he lived. Is that correct?"

Stan Walstrom nodded slowly. "That's correct," he said.

Seemingly, Susie Gray was on a roll and didn't appear to be about to let the opportunity to hammer Walstrom go by. "So it's possible an arrest could have been effected at a later time? Although, I appreciate you didn't know where he was going that night."

Stan Walstrom stood by his actions, saying, "That's correct. However Mr. Michell, as I said earlier, had been involved in a serious incident and we didn't know his state of mind and we couldn't let him go. If we'd have let him go back into town . . . and we didn't know what he was capable of doing that would've been wrong. We didn't want to have anything to further escalate from what was going on."

Susie Gray attempted to solve the apprehension problem for Stan Walstrom by asking, "Have you ever had trouble finding him before . . . when you've tried to locate him?"

Walstrom smiled, he knew Susie Gray wasn't going to like this answer. He remembered the many times he'd gone after Rusty Michell for being unlawfully at large, then he grinned at Susie Gray and said, "Yes, we have, actually."

There was a rustle of laughter throughout the room. Everyone who knew Rusty Michell, knew how he felt about the police.

Susie Gray stopped for a moment; she needed to find another line of questioning. Once again to she turned to the roadblock question, asking, "But I have to ask, one more time, why you couldn't put up a roadblock and simply wait for Mr. Michell to return?"

Stan Walstrom thought to himself that this is going nowhere, but he responded saying, "An apprehension was the only means we had to predict what Mr. Michell was going to do. We wanted to confine him as safely as possible."

Susie Gray pressed on asking, "What would have happened if you had let Mr. Michell go?"

Stan Walstrom's next answer was profound in its simplicity. "If we had let Mr. Michell go . . . we wouldn't have known where he was."

Stan Walstrom let that answer hang in the air for a moment then added, "There were residences in the area and we were worried for the safety of ourselves and the people who lived out there."

Susie Gray avoided the reference to the residences and asked, "You were between him and the town, what advantage was it to continue the pursuit?"

Stan Walstrom waited for a minute. From the look on his face it was clear that he felt nothing he said would satisfy Ms. Gray. Frustrated with the repetitious line of questioning, he replied slowly, "We had to control the situation."

Stan Walstrom was on the stand for an hour. During that time Susie Gray's questions didn't change and neither did Walstrom's answers. When she finally finished and Walstrom was excused, he walked to the opposite side of the Friendship Centre, where steps led up to an open hallway. The hallway led to an upper area with a half wall and a flat railing which Christ'l Roshard had staked out as a press box. Stan Walstrom needed to find a friendly face. He walked over to Christ'l and said, "Geez never again. That's the toughest thing I've ever been through."

That afternoon Stan Walstrom returned to Kamloops with absolutely no remorse about putting as many miles as he could between himself and the whole Rusty Michell affair.

Following the December, 1993 shooting, Walstrom had been transferred to the Kamloops RCMP City Detachment as of May, 1994. He had served four years in Lillooet, the normal length for an RCMP posting and the transfer was expected.

14

AT 9:03 A.M. TUESDAY DECEMBER 13, 1994, Sergeant Al Olsen finally took the stand at the coroner's inquest looking into the death of Russell Thomas Michell. Eleven more days would mark the one-year anniversary of Michell's death.

During that year, Al Olsen had spent a lot of time thinking about the events of that cold Christmas Eve. He thought about the threatening phone calls that followed the shooting and accusations saying it could have been prevented had he acted in a more responsible manner.

As Al Olsen had listened to the extensive questioning of Stan Walstrom and the continual questions about calling off the pursuit, or putting up a road block, he knew his judgment as the commanding officer in this incident was being questioned. But, no matter how he tried to reconstruct the events of that night, he knew there was absolutely no way he could have acted in any other way under those circumstances.

No one had said it, but that night, Russell Michell had the police trapped on the West Pavilion Road. If they had not followed Michell so closely, the hunters would have quickly become the hunted. Michell was breaking the law and leading the police into a setting where he had a clear advantage. There were two sets of rules in play that night, and the rules the police had to play by favored Rusty Michell.

Al Olsen had agonized over the shooting. It was a senseless waste of life, yet there had been no alternative.

Jim Jardine, Al Olsen's counsel, began the questioning by inquiring about Al Olsen's service record with the RCMP. This was followed by questions about the Lillooet tribal police and the events leading up to the phone call from the Kamloops Subdivision. Jardine then got to the pursuit itself and asked Al Olsen about his first assessment of the unfolding events.

Olsen quickly summarized the situation beginning with his stop at the Lillooet RCMP detachment. "After I got my firearm and tried to catch up to Constable Walstrom . . . we had a conversation and he filled me in on what had happened and it became shortly clear that we had a very serious situation with domestic violence, firearms involved . . . possibly children . . . and we felt we had to go on. The subject was known to be violent, he had previous use-of-firearms convictions, he was prohibited from using firearms, he was intoxicated and . . . in my opinion this pursuit really combined all the elements of an extremely serious situation."

Jardine continued: "Were you familiar with him yourself . . . personally?"

Olsen's answer was quick: "Until the Telecoms call that night I'd never met the man nor heard of him before in my life."

Jardine next asked Olsen if he had considered calling off the pursuit. In response to this question, Al Olsen took a few minutes to describe the police car radio system and why all the conversations weren't recorded, including Stan Walstrom's suggestion of a roadblock. This discussion was not on the tape and thus had not been heard by the Coroner's jury. He described the unrecorded conversation and the suggestion of a roadblock: "Specifically, Stan . . . Constable Walstrom asked me about it . . . he said, 'Should we back off and set a road block up?' Considering what we had, I felt there was absolutely no option for that. There was no area that we could possibly set up a road block in safety. I had concern for the members and to a lesser extent I felt that people living in the area could be put at risk if we didn't get him."

Jim Jardine next questioned Al Olsen about the decision to "bump" Michell's car off the road.

Olsen thought for a moment and then slowly went through the series of events that led up to his collision with the green Oldsmobile. "The road conditions actually worked to our benefit at that time. Our speeds were very low on these corners . . . we were doing fifteen K. . . We had fuel problems. No one really seemed to understand or know how much farther we had to go. The best estimate or guess was that we had 60 kilometres to go. For that reason I felt that if the opportunity presented itself, where we can get a sharp corner to the left, it would allow us to bump his vehicle . . . and with any luck at all, his vehicle would slide into the ditch, which would pin the passenger side door . . . which would stop his exit . . and with the police car resting against the other side we would be able to pin the vehicle and bring this to very safe and successful conclusion."

Al continued, first describing Stan Walstrom's loss of control and then the dreadful realization that without backup, he was vulnerable to Rusty Michell's advantage in firepower.

"Once Constable Walstrom went into the ditch, I knew I was in an absolutely terrible position. I didn't dare stop immediately . . . I . . . really at that time, didn't know what I was going to do."

Al paused, vividly recalling the treacherous snow-covered road, the trees on both sides of the road where Michell could take cover and Michell's long-range advantage with his .303 rifle, which could take out Al Olsen with a single shot. His words halted as he recalled the last few minutes of the pursuit.

"Being a single person, I sure didn't want to confront him. The only thing I was thinking at that time was possibly if I could just get him to continue . . . somewhere down the road . . . I could try to come up with . . . a decision. In the final . . . well, the end of the chase happened before I had any real ideas on how I was going to resolve it."

Jim Jardine next asked Al Olsen to describe the weapons involved, "Now tell me Sergeant Olsen, did you have some concerns about the variance in firepower . . . in regards to the rifle versus the firearms that you were carrying and that Constable Walstrom were carrying. Did you have some concerns about that?"

Al was quick to answer. "Oh most definitely. That's one of the major reasons the roadblock was considered out of the question. We could have backed off at some time and set a road block up . . . we could've stood there and he could have walked back at any time and killed us all . . . and we would have had no defence what so ever."

Jim Jardine had to have Al Olsen stress Rusty Michell's firepower advantage for the record and for the benefit of the jury. He continued on the subject, asking, "And why do you say that, perhaps you can explain what was on your mind in regards to the firearms."

Olsen provided the inquest with a quick study in weapons ballistics, at the same time underscoring the superior firepower of Michell's rifle. "The accuracy of a police model revolver is perhaps a maximum of 15 metres. Our shotguns are SSG load, not slug load, therefore maybe 75 yards of some accuracy, probably 40 yards is more accurate. So, with a high-powered rifle, he could stand back at a 100 yards, which is a very accurate range with a rifle . . . and . . . pick us off at will. He also would have the advantage of the dark, while we would be restricted to staying with the vehicle. And there were absolutely no other resources available for backup."

Jardine then took Al Olsen back to the end of the pursuit, asking him to describe the events of the last few minutes.

Al Olsen slowly and thoughtfully told the inquest how the road turned left then right and how he had tried to brake on the icy road before running into the back of Michell's car. Then, he described to the hushed room, the events leading up to the shooting. "The instant I hit him, I looked up and he was already out of his vehicle . . . with the rifle . . . and he had moved into a position at the back."

Al used his hands to describe the collision. Holding his left hand flat, he moved his right hand towards his left, until his index finger hit his left thumb. "His vehicle was like this . . . mine had hit his at that point . . . I looked at him at his face . . . he was yelling . . . he was screaming . . . he immediately lifted the rifle up at me . . . at that point I felt I would be shot . . . there was nothing else I could do . . . I was dead."

Olsen stopped for a minute, then coughed loudly. He was having trouble maintaining composure. "I was reaching for the shotgun in the rack and I'd unlocked the lock . . . and I couldn't get it out." Then there was a longer pause, clearly it wasn't easy for Al to talk about taking a life. Or of the terror that had gripped him as Rusty Michell moved towards the police car.

"Well anyway, I bent down . . . I got below the windshield so that I could try to get some protection from the police car . . . I could see he was coming around to my driver's door . . . I was watching him. . . and at that point I remembered I'd taken my sidearm out and placed it on the passenger's seat . . . as he came around to the side of the car . . . I could see he was in a firing position . . . his hand was down on the trigger area . . . and I felt that as soon as he became level with the window of the door . . . he was going to begin firing." Al Olsen stopped again to compose himself. Then, showing less emotion than he had earlier, he described the shooting. "I didn't bother trying to roll the window down . . . I just rolled around with my revolver . . . I don't know how many shots I fired initially . . . I just started pulling the trigger . . . and aiming at the form I could see through the glass . . . through all the firing and the glass flying I had a recollection that I was moving up and around as I was firing."

At that point, Al Olsen's throat began to tighten again, he paused, coughed again to clear his throat, then continued. "I think I wrote originally that I'd hit him in the side and the back." Al was having a difficult time continuing. He cleared his throat and tried to go on. "Since then . . . since then . . . I think I've clarified in my mind that when

I looked out . . . he was still on his hands and knees getting up again . . . he still had the rifle. I reached out . . . I pulled the trigger and one round went off and at that point it was clicking empty."

Olsen then described how he got out of the car and yelled at Rusty Michell to drop the gun and roll over. He told of seeing blood in the snow and when they opened his shirt, the wound at his left nipple. "When he wasn't responsive to our calls . . . we got an emergency blanket and covered him . . . and a few minutes later he passed away."

Next Al Olsen told the courtroom how he had briefed Stan Walstrom on taking charge of the scene and ensuring that Stan Walstrom wrote down every observation he made.

Jim Jardine then asked Al Olsen to describe the similar shooting incident that had occurred three year earlier at the Pinchie Reserve. This allowed Al Olsen to speak of the damage that occurs in RCMP/native relationships when a shooting happens.

He went on at some length about attempting to wait it out with Randy Monk, but in the end, when lives were threatened, how Randy Monk had to be taken down. Al Olsen concluded, saying, "Having gone through the experience at Pinchie, I knew that night that although this was over and Michell was dead, it was only just beginning, the worst was yet to come for the community, the police, my family, everybody."

Now it was Renee Taylor's turn to question Al Olsen. She began with the same line of questioning that Susie Gray had put to Constable Stan Walstrom the day before, first questioning Al Olsen about his knowledge of the area and whether or not there were residences where the shooting had taken place. Al responded by saying he knew there were some ranches in that area. One not too far from the scene.

Taylor then asked about the possibility that Michell might be able to get out of sight, leave his vehicle and come back to Lillooet on foot through the snow. Al Olsen responded by simply saying that the area in question was reasonably flat and he had no idea how deep the snow was. He left the jury and Ms. Taylor to sort out that scenario.

However, Renee Taylor seemed determined to demonstrate that Al Olsen had not used good judgement that evening. She next questioned Olsen's decision to push Michell off the road, saying, "On that particular road at that time of night, in the adverse weather conditions that were prevailing, how sensible was it to bump . . . to elect to bump the vehicle?"

Al Olsen knew his plan to put Michell's car in the snowbank would have been the best, and safest way to end the chase. He answered quickly, "Oh I still think it was a very wise decision, we were in a situation where it was very safe, contact was not difficult . . . if it had went the right way . . . probably Mr. Michell would be alive today." (Appendix J)

Ruth Taylor wasn't at all satisfied with that answer and continued to question Al Olsen's judgment. "You say that when Walstrom's vehicle got stuck you didn't want to stop to give Mr. Michell any distance . . . you didn't want him to get away."

Al Olsen grabbed at this question. It gave him a good opening to explain the difficulty of the situation. "My worry then was that if I stopped to pick up Stan and Keith, I would then lose contact. . . if you lose contact . . . you lose control . . . it may not have been very good control

. . . but what little of what we had, we knew what he was doing . . . as long as we could see him.

"Uh huh." Taylor nodded and said nothing more.

Al Olsen continued, "If I'd stopped there, considering his state, his history with his alcohol problems, there's nothing saying he wouldn't have stopped his vehicle walked up from his car and blown us away. It's the same problem I had with the roadblock. I didn't know what I was going to do but I knew I had to get some distance between our members stuck in the ditch and Mr. Michell."

Renee Taylor stuck to her line of questioning about stopping for the other two officers, "I know it's hindsight now, but being realistic, how long would it have taken for you to stop your vehicle, have Walstrom and McKay jump in and carry on? Seconds?"

Al didn't hesitate to answer, he responded quickly, almost spitting out every word. "Long enough that we could have been dead!" Al Olsen let the word "dead" sink in, then he continued, "It was not a good move. I would never recommend stopping and I would never do it!"

Renee Taylor tried to downplay the deadly seriousness of Olsen's answer. She asked, "Are we looking at seconds?"

Al fired back, "Fifteen seconds, twenty seconds, in hindsight whatever, five seconds is too long, the minute you've lost sight, you've lost control."

Taylor wouldn't drop this line of questioning, "But you will agree with me it wouldn't have taken long."

Al thought to himself, Geez, what's long? Then he answered, "Not knowing if they were still in their seat belts, it could have taken ten seconds to fifty seconds. I had no idea."

"But we're not talking about a long period of time."

"We're talking about a period of time that would have put Mr. Michell hundreds of yards away from us . . . that's loss of sight."

Taylor continued, "In layman's language we're talking seconds?"

Al shrugged, he didn't answer, but thought, that's a dumb question, when are "seconds" in layman's language?

Renee Taylor wouldn't let go. "Looking at it now, if you had the backup, if you had one of the other officers that were with you . . .

Al Olsen had had enough, he interrupted Taylor and said, "I couldn't consider it . . . I would have loved to have the backup but if I would've stopped, I would have put those members lives at risk and I couldn't do that."

There was a long delay. Taylor was searching. "Was there a time when you thought of calling off the chase?"

Al's response was rapid, almost to the point of cutting off Taylor's question before she was finished. Quickly he shot back, "No. At no time that whole evening did we ever consider calling off the chase. I felt strongly that if we'd have called it off . . . Mr. Michell's family was at great risk."

Taylor wasn't having any of this, she pressed on about safeguarding Kathy James. "Could you have not protected the family by putting an officer at the house? And then awaited for Mr. Michell to come down that mountain?"

Again Al's response was quick and to the point. "But we still would have had the same problem we had before, if he came back down that mountain . . . when is he going to come . . . where he's going to come . . . and . . . how is he going to come."

Renee Taylor continued to press Al Olsen on his decision to stay with Michell. She said, "Now sizing up this situation, we have the road and the weather conditions, we have insufficient gas, in testimony given yesterday we heard that people were running low on petrol . . . there's increasing vulnerability for the members the farther down the road . . . the members go . . . to isolating themselves further . . . the darkness. Do you think any of those factors could weigh in the balance in the decision to continue the pursuit?"

Al was quick to answer: "No I did not."

Then he paused. He thought of his twenty years on the police force, much of it dealing with the terrible abuse that occurs on native reserves. He thought of the battered women and children he'd seen. The eyes swollen shut from beatings, the broken noses, the black and blue faces, painful testimony to the brutality that happens when natives drown their problems in alcohol. In twenty years he'd seen it all.

By now Al Olsen was glaring at Taylor. He had made the right decision that night and he was not going to have his decision questioned by someone who hadn't the faintest understanding of the seriousness of spousal abuse.

He spoke slowly, yet sternly, letting every word sink in. The large Native Friendship centre was hushed as he described his feelings that evening. "The easiest decision I could have made that night . . . was to call off the pursuit. I would have loved to have been home with my family and pretended this incident never happened. But . . . I could never live with myself if Mrs. Michell . . . or any of her family were killed . . . because of that decision."

Renee Taylor was taken aback by Al Olsen's terse response. She looked at him, then changed the subject and asked if the RCMP spousal abuse policy had been discussed by any of the officers during the pursuit. The answer was no. Ruth Taylor had no more questions.

Al Olsen was excused. At long last, for Al Olsen at least, the Russell Michell inquest was over.

STNP Constable Keith McKay was the last police officer to appear at the inquest. Most of the questions to McKay came from Renee Taylor who continued with the same line of cross examination put previously to Al Olsen and Stan Walstrom.

Taylor spent most of her time with McKay insisting that the pursuit could have been called off. Keith McKay would have none of it, explaining over and over again, "If we had lost sight of Michell, we would have lost control." Taylor could see that her questions were going nowhere, she sat down.

The long awaited inquest into the shooting of Russell Thomas Michell was finally winding down.

15

THE NEXT WITNESS TO TESTIFY at the coroner's inquest was Rusty Michell's foster father Fred John. Fred was a loving and deeply spiritual man, who spoke openly of Russell's troubled youth. At the end of his statement he touched on his own youth, relating it to Rusty Michell's upbringing, it was a moving testament to the tragic history of native people.

Following his swearing in as a witness, Fred John calmly took the stand. A handsome, soft-spoken man in his seventies, Fred told of the Indian tradition that views crime as a sickness, one that is treated with its own type of healing. It was a powerful insight into Russell Michell's life, and as Fred John began talking he touched the hearts of everyone in the room.

Slowly Fred John began his testimony, saying, "When Russell first came to live with us, I knew he was a troubled boy. He'd go up into the mountains, in our traditional way this is how we heal. We heal with the mountains . . . with the living things around us. And this is what he'd do, he'd do this and come back, and he feel really better, and he'd thank me . . . he'd apologize . . . and this is how he got rid of a lot of his frustrations. Because he couldn't talk too much to people, he didn't know how to . . . you know . . . express himself, but he always dealt with things in that way.

As years went by, he came to me and talked to me and we related a lot of things that really . . . meant a lot.

And that night, I believed . . . when I . . . I was sure then this was happening, when they mentioned that the gun was not loaded, I knew that already. Because when Russell went out, he didn't have his gun loaded a lot of times. I mean all the time I knew him he wouldn't load his gun in the vehicle. Only when he got out to go hunting, then he would go out and load the gun and do the hunting.

In one of his frustration times, he would take his rifle and go . . . he would stay out into the mountains. And I believe that on this night, when he was on his way out of town, I believe that's where he was heading. He was going to go out and just be alone for a while to release his frustrations . . . It didn't turn out that way. And when I saw the gun, that it wasn't loaded, I knew that . . . that to be alone was one of the purposes of what he was doing.

But he was a happy, friendly, loving person when he was with us. And he used to tell my son Dave . . . he used to tell him secrets like he didn't want anyone to know he was a soft easy-going guy because he had to prove that he was such a hard case. And he used to tell Dave that when he'd go out he used to have to demonstrate the other way of life, that he had to prove himself . . . prove himself to the world. But I really had a lot of trust in him, a lot of faith, he loved his family, loved his children and he was grateful for having that chance to have a family and children.

And he'd come to me and tell me that, he would say, I'm doing OK now. But there was still that doubt that he had in himself, or around him, things weren't quite OK that he couldn't forget a lot of the past . . . that had really damaged his upbringing . . . what ever it was."

The large main room of the Lillooet Native Friendship Centre was hushed. Fred John was speaking slowly and more thoughtfully. He seemed to be having a difficult time putting together what he wanted to say next. He took a deep breath, which seemed to relax him. He went on, speaking openly of the shame kept silent for so many years by the Indians, the Roman Catholic Church and the various authorities. It was a quiet, yet gripping reference to the abuse that Russell Michell and so many other young Indians had suffered for many years.

"He had a hard life when he was young, a very, very hard life. But like I said at the beginning . . . when a child is . . . anything below thirteen, that's how you're going to be. . . . and you know you'll have a hard time to erase that . . . the memories of those kinds of things."

"The residential schools . . . all of the things that happen on the reserves . . . 'cause I went through a lot of that myself. I understood what he was talking about. Because I was . . . I was . . . a victim . . . of those kind of ways.

A lot of Indian people do have a very . . . very hard time dealing with that and with the RCMP, and to lay these things aside." Then, surprisingly, Fred John spoke positively of the way the RCMP had changed their attitude towards the Indian people and the positive changes that had been made. "It was good . . . a few years ago when the RCMP Detachment came up to join us in our sweat lodge at Fountain. Really we felt good . . . one of our elders said he did not think he'd live to see the day when this would ever happen. And that was good . . . it was a good step."

Fred John, ever the peacemaker answered a few concluding questions from Coroner Bob Graham and then stepped down from the witness stand. His simple yet eloquent testimony had taken less than five minutes, but his words, with their dignity and honesty, had bared over one hundred years of bigotry and abuse.

James Malone, one of the investigators hired by the Bridge River Band to look into the shooting and provide a background check on Rusty Michell, was the last witness to take the stand. Malone had been asked by the Bridge River Band to speak to the inquest about his investigation into Michell's character.

James Malone began by saying that although Rusty had numerous run-ins with the law, he was considered to be a loyal friend, a good father and dependable. Malone stressed that since Rusty subsidized his income by hunting, it wouldn't be unusual for him to be carrying a rifle in his car. Malone said that he had checked with Lillooet bar owners and had found that Rusty Michell had never been barred from any of the local pubs.

He concluded by saying, "So the reputation on one side . . . you get a picture of the last two hours of a man's life . . . and he represented a lot more than that . . . and the family wants that to be known. He had one of the largest funerals attended out in this area and the family wanted me to come up and make sure that as a person from the outside . . . that didn't know him personally . . . that I interviewed a lot of people in town and . . . there was a lot of good things said about Rusty Michell." With that said, Malone sat down.

Coroner Bob Graham began his closing comments to the jury with a snapshot review of the events leading to Rusty's death. Graham started with Kathy James' phone call, then moved on to the police response and pursuit, and finally the shooting. His purpose was to summarize for the record all the evidence the jury had heard during the course of the inquest.

Still aware of the underlying suspicion towards Al Olsen and the RCMP, Bob Graham once again stressed the role of the jury in a coroner's inquest, saying, "You must be careful in rendering a verdict that you do not find fault or blame with anyone. This is not a civil or a criminal court, it is simply a fact-finding body."

Graham then provided a more technical summary, identifying the deceased as Russell Thomas Michell, giving Rusty's age at the time of death, specifying where the death occurred, what the autopsy had shown as the cause of death and advising the jury that they would have to determine the exact time of death from the RCMP transcripts.

Bob Graham gave his final instructions to the jury, "You are required also, for the purposes of Vital Statistics, to classify the death. You have several choices there, and I need to expand on the science of those choices. First obviously, is death by natural causes . . . and I don't believe that anyone has suggested he died by natural causes."

Graham paused. He knew the members of the Bridge River Band were hanging on every word. "You have the opportunity then to look at the unnatural classifications which are available to you. First of those is an accidental death. And that's a death which results from actions by a person which causes their own death. Or death that result from the intervention of non-human means."

Bob Graham stopped again, as if to give the jury a moment to sort out the various classifications. After a brief pause he continued. "Secondly, you have the option of ruling the death to be a suicide. And that's a death which results primarily from self-inflicted injury, with an apparent self-intent to cause the death of the individual."

At this point, Coroner Bob Graham made an intriguing observation, not at all lost on Al Olsen, who recalled Randy Monk's behavior on the night he was shot at the Pinchie Reserve. "There is a school of thought, and we probably could have called a psychologist here, because certainly there are documented cases where people take their own lives by charging towards an armed police officer, with a weapon. Those deaths in fact are ruled as suicide. We have no way of determining what the intent of Mr. Michell was as he approached that vehicle."

Bob Graham then made an observation that was uncharacteristic of him, suggesting that Rusty knew his rifle clip had dropped out on the floor of the car. "Rusty Michell would have known if that rifle was unloaded. I can't give you any explanation, and neither can any of the witnesses who were here as to why he was approaching that police car."

Jim Jardine, Al Olsen's counsel, was taken aback at this comment, Graham's making some pretty big assumptions here, he thought. But he let it go.

Bob Graham also seemed to sense he was on dangerous ground and backed away from his earlier suggestion. He now said, "My opinion as to whether it was a suicide or not, is not important, because that's your decision. But I would suggest there's not a lot of evidence . . . there's not a preponderance of evidence to suggest that he intended to end his life by walking toward a police car with that rifle."

All the RCMP officers in the room knew that anyone walking towards a police car and pointing a rifle had clearly established intent. And they would bring about a justifiably predictable outcome.

Bob Graham moved on to the next classification, with this description: "The next option with respect to classification of death is that of homicide." Graham knew the impact this term had on the room and he spent a considerable amount of time explaining the meaning of homicide, particularly as it applied to Al Olsen and the actions that led to Rusty Michell's death.

"Homicide is defined in the Criminal Code of Canada as a death which results directly, or indirectly, by the actions of another person." Bob Graham paused again. He felt it was critical to stress the meaning of the term homicide as it applied to the inquest.

"Homicide is just that neutral in the Criminal Code and it doesn't imply fault or blame. It simply says he died at the hands of another person. The Code goes on to further define homicide as culpable or non-culpable. It is there where we get into the areas of intent and this coroner's inquest does not need to get into that area. Culpable homicide is murder or manslaughter. The representative here from the Attorney General's Ministry has had the opportunity to review the file, and officials from the Attorney General's Ministry have clearly decided that there is not sufficient evidence for them to proceed with any charges regarding culpable homicide. So that's why Sergeant Olsen is not charged with a criminal offence. Nevertheless, it is not improper for you to rule the death to be a homicide, if you believe that he fully intended to take Mr. Michell's life when the incident took place. You don't need to . . . feel badly about that . . . the word homicide tends to get a lot of play because it's used so often on television and other areas and in the media areas of our society."

Here Bob Graham began to repeat himself, but he had to make the point that a verdict of homicide did not imply that Al Olsen had acted with criminal intent. Slowly, Graham explained the meaning again, saying, "Homicide itself is clearly quite a neutral term, it simply means death caused by the actions of another person, without going into intent, or state of mind."

"If you are unable from the evidence you've heard here to make a determination with respect to the classification of death, you may rule the death to be undetermined. And there are two ways in which you may want to arrive at that: Either you don't feel there was sufficient evidence to classify what you've got, or . . . you feel that the death could have been just as easily classified as an accident, a suicide, or a homicide, or anything else. And the weight and the balance of it so that you can't determine one way or another if it was an accident, a suicide or a homicide. Then in those circumstances, you may also determine the death to be undetermined and classify it that way."

Bob Graham continued his closing remarks by advising the jury that they would be provided with all the exhibits presented during the inquest. He added that the jury would be given copies of RCMP policy on spousal assault, hazardous pursuits and the use of deadly force. He then said, "You are sequestered into the custody of the Sheriff and you are to remain together until such time as you have rendered a verdict. In addition to the facts of the verdict you may make recommendations if you feel they would prevent future loss of life under similar circumstances. If there are any issues you wish to make recommendations on, you may do so." He concluded, saying, "Mr. Foreman, if you have any questions that need further clarification, or if you wish to call back witnesses, advise Mr. Sheriff and we'll assist you in any way we can."

The jury filed out to a private room behind the large public area of the Friendship Centre. Twenty minutes later they returned, but only to ask for a written copy of the various classifications of death.

An hour passed before they returned again. Bob Graham reconvened the inquest, looked at foreman Dave Horne and said, "If you are all in agreement, Mr. Foreman would you read the verdict."

Jury Foreman Dave Horne rose, holding the handwritten verdict in his hand, he began to read: " We the jury find that Russell Thomas Michell came to his death at approximately 21:35 hours on the 24th day of December, 1993 at, or near 67.5 kilometres on the West Pavilion Road. We find that the medical cause of death blood loss and trauma as result of gunshot wounds."

Dave Horne paused, then said, "We the Jury classify the death as homicide."

Coroner Bob Graham asked if the Jury had any findings or recommendations as a result of the inquest.

Dave Horne said, "Yes we do."

Bob Graham asked Dave Horne to read the recommendations.

Horne continued. "We the Jury recommend the following: One: Once the safety of all persons was assured, general first aid practices respecting the rights and welfare of the suspect be provided. From the evidence presented, we were not able to determine whether appropriate first aid was given.

"Two: We feel that increased familiarity with the jurisdictional area would have assisted the officers. For example: have officers travel main routes and be familiar with the population.

"Three: Kamloops Telecoms should have available current maps and access to a list of local contacts for additional information about rural roads. "We recommend that the Kamloops Section Commanding Officer of the RCMP take the above recommendations into consideration."

The members of the Bridge River Band sat quietly as Foreman Dave Horne finished reading the recommendations and took his seat. They had wanted more from this inquest. One of their own was dead at the hands of a police officer. In their minds the pursuit should have been called off. Rusty would have sobered up and he would still be alive. It was a senseless killing, but all the jury recommended was better maps and more familiarity with rural roads. Al Olsen was alive and Russell Michell was dead. It wasn't right. Bob Graham ended the coroner's inquest by thanking the jury. Kathy James left the Native Friendship Centre. She felt empty. She didn't know what she had expected out of the inquest, but nothing had changed.

Al Olsen left the Friendship Centre and returned immediately to Kamloops. He remained with the commercial crime unit until June, 1995 when he was promoted to the rank of Staff Sergeant and was given a new position at the Kamloops City Detachment as an operations commander.

The next day the RCMP returned Rusty's clothes to Kathy. RCMP procedure calls for keeping the clothes of a deceased person when a coroner's inquest has been called. The clothes, even blood-stained clothes, are hung up to dry in well ventilated storage. Following an inquest, the clothes are returned.

It was important for Kathy to have Rusty's clothes, as it's a native custom to burn the clothes a deceased person was wearing at the time of death. Sagebrush is also burned, to purify the soul. Rusty's clothes had been hung up on hangers to dry. Kathy wept when she took them off the hangers and saw the blood-stained T-shirt and long underwear bottoms. Two small holes in the back of the underwear were dramatic testimony to a tough life and a tragic death.

That Saturday afternoon, December 17, surrounded by friends and family, Kathy burned Rusty's clothes in a fire pit. The burning sagebrush sweetened the air with its light perfume. The smoke from the fire they had lit to burn Rusty's clothes rose in the air, at first thick and dark. Then as it rose higher and higher, it drifted, turning and twisting, becoming lighter. Then it was gone, disappearing into the trees, the mountains and the sky — escaping and at last finding freedom.

Appendix A

STANDARD 10 - CODE

10-4 Acknowledgement	10-46 Person in Prohibited
10-6 Busy	Category
10-7 Out of Service	10-61 Coffee Break
10-8 In Service	10-62 Meal Break
10-9 Repeat	10-65 Escorting Prisoner
10-10 Negative	10-66 Prisoner Transport
10-14 Prepare to Copy	Required
10-20 Location	10-67 Unauthorized
10-23 Arrived at Scene	Listener Present
10-27 Drivers Licence Infor-	10-68 Breathalyzer
mation Required	Operator Required
10-28 Vehicle Registration	10-69 Checking Vehicle /
Information Required	Person
10-29 Check Records for	10-72 Alarm or Serious
Vehicle or Subject	Crime
10-30 Danger / Caution	10-75 Change Frequencies
10-33 Officer in Trouble	10-80 Record of Violence
10-40 Possible Hit on	10-81 Record of Robbery
10-41 Possible Hit now	10-82 Record of Offensive
Confirmed with	Weapon
Originating Agency	10-83 Record of B & E
10-42 Person / Vehicle in	10-84 Record of Theft
Observation Category	10-85 Record of Drugs
10-43 Person in Parole	10-86 Record of Fraud
Category	10-87 Record of Sex
10-44 Person in Charged	10-88 Record of Other
Category	Criminal Code
10-45 Person in Elopee	10-89 Record of Arson
Category	

Appendix B

Letter	Word	Pronounced As
A	Alfa	al fa
B	Bravo	brah voh
C	Charlie	char lee
D	Delta	dell tah
E	Echo	eck oh
F	Foxtrot	foks trot
G	Golf	golf
H	Hotel	hoh tell
I	India	in dee ah
J	Juliette	jew lee ette
K	Kilo	key loh
L	Lima	lee mah
M	Mike	mike
N	November	no vem ber
O	Oscar	oss cah
P	Papa	pah pah
Q	Quebec	keh beck
R	Romeo	row me oh
S	Sierra	see air rah
T	Tango	tang go
U	Uniform	you nee form
V	Victor	vic tah
W	Whiskey	wiss key
X	X-ray	ecks ray
Y	Yankee	yang key
Z	Zulu	zoo loo

Appendix C

news release communiqué

Royal Canadian Mounted Police   Gendarmerie royale du Canada

not to be released before: *ne pas publier avant:*
93.12.30

FATAL SHOOTING - LILLOOET RCMP

ON 93.12.24 AT 1942 HOURS, THE KAMLOOPS R.C.M.P. OPERATIONAL
COMMUNICATIONS CENTRE RECEIVED A CALL FROM A DISTRAUGHT
FEMALE. THE CALLER COMPLAINED ABOUT HER COMMON-LAW HUSBAND,
RUSTY MICHELL, WITH RESPECT TO HIS ATTEMPTING TO TAKE HER FIVE
CHILDREN WITHOUT PERMISSION. SHE ADVISED THAT RUSTY MICHELL
HAD TRASHED THE HOUSE AND WAS IN AN INEBRIATED CONDITION AND
WAS IN POSSESSION OF A WEAPON, A HUNTING RIFLE.

AT 1954 HOURS, CST. WALSTROM OF LILLOOET R.C.M.P. AND CST.
McKAY OF S.N.T.P. LOCATED RUSTY MICHELL ON THE WEST PAVILION
ROAD AND ATTEMPTED TO STOP HIS VEHICLE. MICHELL IGNORED THESE
ATTEMPTS AND CONTINUED TO DRIVE NORTH ON THE WEST PAVILION
ROAD IN A HAPHAZARD MANNER. HE WAS ALONE IN THE VEHICLE.

AT 2006 HOURS, SGT. AL OLSEN, NCO I/C LILLOOET DETACHMENT, WAS
CONTACTED AT HIS RESIDENCE AND ADVISED OF THE ONGOING PURSUIT.
SGT. OLSEN IMMEDIATELY DEPARTED HIS RESIDENCE TO JOIN THE
PURSUIT AND CAUGHT UP TO THE CHASE AT THE 60 KM. MARK.

.../CONTINUED

Canada

Appendix C (continued)

news release communiqué

Royal Canadian Mounted Police   Gendarmerie royale du Canada

not to be released before: *ne pas publier avant:*

93.12.30 - PAGE 2

FATAL SHOOTING - LILLOOET RCMP

AT THE 67 KM MARK, CST. WALSTROM LOST CONTROL OF HIS VEHICLE
AND WAS IMMOBILIZED IN THE DITCH. SGT. OLSEN CONTINUED THE
PURSUIT AND AT THE 67.6 KM MARK HE CAME UPON MICHELL'S
VEHICLE, STATIONARY AND SIDEWAYS ON THE ROAD. SGT. OLSEN'S
POLICE TRANSPORT HIT THE MICHELL VEHICLE, THE LEFT FRONT OF
THE POLICE VEHICLE CAME IN CONTACT WITH THE RIGHT REAR FENDER
OF MICHELL'S VEHICLE.

BEFORE IMPACT, RUSTY MICHELL HAD ALIGHTED FROM HIS VEHICLE.
WHEN SGT. OLSEN'S VEHICLE CAME TO REST, HE WAS CONFRONTED BY
RUSTY MICHELL, POINTING A 30/30 RIFLE AT HIM THROUGH THE LEFT
FRONT DRIVER'S WINDOW. AT THIS POINT, SGT. OLSEN LEANED
BACKWARDS, WITH HIS SERVICE REVOLVER DRAWN, AND COMMENCED
FIRING THROUGH THE CLOSED WINDOW. MICHELL WAS STRUCK BY THREE
BULLETS AND WAS FATALLY WOUNDED.

AN INDEPENDENT R.C.M.P. COMMISSIONED OFFICER HAS BEEN ASSIGNED
TO OVERSEE THE INVESTIGATION AND A CORONER'S INQUEST IS
PENDING. A REPORT ON THE MATTER WILL BE SUBMITTED TO THE
CROWN COUNSEL FOR THEIR REVIEW AND RECOMMENDATION.

- 30 -

Canada

Appendix D

BRIDGE RIVER INDIAN BAND

P.O. BOX 190, LILLOOET, B.C.   V0K 1V0   256-7423

January 5, 1994

Herbert Gray
Solicitor General of Canada
Parliament Buildings
Ottowa, Ontario

Colin Gableman, Minister
Attorney General of British Columbia
Parliament Buildings
Victoria, B.C.

Dear Mr. Minister:

As you know, on Christmas Eve, Thirty-one year old Russell Thomas Michell, father of five children, a Stl'atl'imx citizen from Bridge River was fatally shot by a Sergeant A.B. Olsen a member of your contract police, the Royal Canadian Mounted Police.

As you also know, it has been repeated in local, regional and national press reports that Sergeant A.E. Olsen did not have a choice but to shoot and kill Mr. Michell 67.5 kilometres up the Slok Creek forestry road. It is the contention of the Bridge River Band that the shooting was preventable had a more responsible decision been made by the officer in charge.

Mr. Minister, I am aware of the internal investigation currently underway and of a coroners inquest in the near future. However, because the R.C.M.P. deny (press statements) they had a choice in the outcome, it appears they (R.C.M.P.) have arrived at a conclusion in the incident without benefit of the above processes. It is the view of the Bridge River Band that a full public inquiry be held on this issue, not withstanding the up coming release of the findings on the Oppal Commission.

Furthermore, on January 4th, 1994 at the request of myself, a meeting of local Chiefs, Councillors and our citizens together with visitors from other Indian Nations was held in Lillooet. At our meeting, after much deliberation, a call for a Federal and Provincial Royal Commission mandated to examine the relationship between your police forces, especially the Royal Canadian Mounted Police, the B.C. Justice system and Indian Nations be established.

.2/

Appendix D (continued)

Pg.2/Gableman/Jan 5/94

The rationale for such a call is the shooting of Russell Michell and the facts surrounding the action or inaction of police in the traumatic disappearance of Lenore Napoleon last seen on the night of Russell's shooting (on Christmas Eve). Many other disturbing incidents across the Province indicate the need for a Royal Commission, and numerous incidents in Sti'atl'imx Territory demand that you heed our call and I trust that your offices will respond positively.

Yours truly,

Chief Saul Terry

Councillor

Councillor

Councillor
Bridge River Indian Band

CST:ft

CC: Hon. Jean Chretian, Prime Minister of Canada
Mr. Ron Irwin, Federal Minister of Indian Affairs
Ethel Blondin-Andrews, M.P. Secretary of State
Senator Len Marchand
Elijah Harper, M.P.
Union of B.C. Indian Chiefs

Appendix E

P.O. Box 3068 - 35710 Langley-Lillooet Tel: (604) 820-2517 Fax: (604) 820-9435

January 07, 1994.

VIA FAX.

RECEIVED
OFFICE OF THE
ATTORNEY GENERAL
SAMSOB
JAN 0 7 1994
REFER TO MAIL REGISTRY ☐
OTHER _____
☑ DRAFT REPLY
☐ ATTN. FILE   FILE ☐   REPLY DIRECT ☐
    INFORMATION ☐

TO: The Bridge River Indian Band
    P.O. Box 190,
    Lilloet, B.C. V0K 1V0

FROM: Chief Clarke Smith
      Samahquam Band
      P.O. Box 3068
      Mission, B.C. V2V 4J3.

Chief Saul Terry.

RE: Russell Thomas Michell-Deceased.

On Behalf of the People of Samahquam, we offer our sympathy to the immediat family' for their loss.

We support you, in your quest for some Measure of Justice relating to the shooting incident, by the RCMP, that took the life of your citizen Russell Thomas Michell. Yes, there are many questions to be answered regarding this incident. Yes, there is a definite need for the Government of Canada and B.C. to review the poor relationship that exist between the Police Forces and the Aboriginal Communities.

It has been twenty years, since similar events took place on a road between Risky Creek and Anihim Reserve at which time eventually the Life of one Fred Quilt expired. Again, the R.C.M.P. handled the situation. Numerous other Aboriginal Communities across this Country called Canada, have been faced with similar events, ending with the same results, the Justice System does not care whether or not the Aboriginal People receive Fair and Equitable Treatment by their Police Forces.

-2-

Appendix E (continued)

Jan. 07, 1994.

Chief Saul Terry
Bridge River Band.

Chief Saul Terry, we agree with you and the Chiefs that a Royal
Commission be charged with the responsibility of examining the
relationships between the Canadian Police Forces (especially the
Royal Canadian Mounted Police) the B.C. Justice System and the
Indian People. However, we would like to add that it is time
to Request the United Nations, Human Rights Commissions to get
involved in such a Commission. Remember the Perpetrators are the
ones that built Canadian Law, do you think that they will be
at all. fair, since they are the ones on the hot seat?

Keep us posted, thank you. Let the Creator Guide us all.

All my Relations.

Chief Clarke Smith.

cc. Stl'atl'imx Chiefs
    National Chief AFN
    The Honorable Colin Gableman
      Min. Attorney Gen. B.C.
    First Nations Summitt
    Stolo Nation Canada.
    Caribou Tribal Council
    Human Rights Commisssions United Nations.

Appendix F

FEB 21 1994

RECEIV

FEB 22 1994

POLICY AND RESOURCE ANALYSIS
BRANCH

Chief Saul Terry
Bridge River Indian Band
P.O. Box 190
Lillooet, British Columbia
V0K 1V0

Dear Chief Terry:

Thank you for your letter of January 5, 1994, on the death
of Mr. Russell Thomas Michell.

I appreciate the seriousness of your concerns over this
incident and extend my sympathy to all Stl'atl'imx citizens
affected by it.

As you mention in your letter, the Royal Canadian Mounted
Police is conducting an investigation into the shooting.
The R.C.M.P. will forward the report of their investigation
to Crown Counsel of the Criminal Justice Branch of the
Ministry of Attorney General for their independent
consideration of possible criminal charges.

I note your request for a public inquiry into this incident.
In fact, the coroner's inquest to which you refer will
provide the appropriate forum to examine the issues raised
by Mr. Michell's death. The inquest will be public and will
inquire into all circumstances of his death. It is within
the coroner's jurisdiction to make recommendations regarding
any other matters arising out of the inquest, including the
justice system's treatment of aboriginal people.

In addition, as you know, the Cariboo-Chilcotin Justice
Inquiry looked at the broader issues of the justice system's
treatment of aboriginal people along with the specific
concerns of the aboriginal people of the Cariboo-Chilcotin
region.

I stated publicly on releasing Judge Anthony Sarich's report
of the inquiry that the government will discuss the report's
implications with aboriginal communities, the R.C.M.P.

Province of   Attorney General   Parliament Buildings
British Columbia   Victoria, British Columbia
                                          V8V 1X4

Appendix F (continued)

Chief Terry
Page 2

provincial ministers of justice, the federal government, and
British Columbia's Chief Justices and Chief Judge. Indeed,
the ongoing reform of the justice system is part of the
provincial government's larger vision of justice for
aboriginal people.

I trust this information is helpful.

Yours sincerely,

Original Signed by

Colin Gabelmann
Attorney General

cc: Chief Clarke Smith
     Honourable Jean Chretian
     Honourable Ethel Blondin-Andrews
     Senator Len Marchand
     Union of B.C. Indian Chiefs
     Mr. Elijah Harper, M.P.
     Mr. Ron Irwin

THOMPSON:cg

Appendix G

 **Province of British Columbia** | Ministry of Attorney General | **NEWS RELEASE**

Criminal Justice Branch
Ministry of Attorney General
May 4, 1994   94:22

CROWN ANNOUNCES CHARGING DECISION IN MICHELL CASE

LILLOOET -- No criminal charges will be laid against a member of the Lillooet RCMP following the death of Russell Thomas Michell on December 24, 1993 near Lillooet, southern interior regional Crown Counsel Hermann Rohrmoser announced today.

Rohrmoser announced his decision after a review of a Report to Crown Counsel prepared by police on the fatal shooting of Michell. Michell was shot following a domestic violence complaint and a police chase.

The circumstances in the case have been carefully reviewed by Rohrmoser, and by Peter Ewert, Q.C., Director, Special Programs, Environmental Law and Aboriginal Justice of the Criminal Justice Branch in Victoria. Their consensus is that the police officer acted in self-defence and without criminal intent.

On May 4, 1994, Rohrmoser, Regional Coroner Robert Graham and a senior RCMP officer met with members of the family and other interested members of the Lillooet community to explain the Crown's decision that charges would not be laid.

No further comment will be made about the circumstances of the case at this time in view of the Coroner's Inquest set for June 22, 1994 before Regional Coroner Graham.

- 30 -

Contact:
Hermann Rohrmoser
Regional Crown Counsel
Tel: 828-4021 (Kamloops)

General Media Inquiries:
Donna Sitter
Tel: 387-5008 (Victoria)

Appendix H

BRIDGE RIVER INDIAN BAND
P.O. BOX 190, LILLOOET, B.C. V0K 1V0 256-7423

Chief Saul Terry
Bridge River Indian Band

At the announcement of the inquest date the Bridge River Band requested that finances be provided to our people to prepare ourselves for the inquiry.

On June 20th, two days before the commencement of the inquest we indicated that proper finances have not been made available and therefore a fair and equitable hearing would not be possible. Our message to the Coroner, Mr. Robert Graham was that due to this circumstance there would not have been any justice to the Russell Michell family and the Indian Community in general.

With the postponement of the Coroner's Inquest we have a further opportunity to acquire resources which would make possible a more fair, equitable and just hearing on the shooting incident of December 24, 1993 where Russell Thomas Michell was fatally shot.

-30-

Appendix I

E. **INVESTIGATIVE TECHNIQUES** (cont'd)

E. 5. b. **Member**

1. Do not start a pursuit with a nonpolice passenger in the police vehicle. An auxiliary constable on duty is a police passenger.

2. Drive with due regard for the safety of other motorists and pedestrians.

3. Use all the emergency warning equipment with which the vehicle is equipped.

   1. In a hazardous pursuit situation, you must use only a fully marked police vehicle equipped with a roof light bar, siren and revolving lamps.

   2. You may only use an unmarked, clean-roof police vehicle in a hazardous pursuit if it is absolutely necessary to protect life.

4. Before initiating or continuing a hazardous pursuit, consider the following:

   1. if the subject is known or can be identified, whether apprehension can be effected at some later time;

   2. the age of the driver and the manner in which he/she is operating the vehicle;

   3. apprehension by other means, e.g. requesting assistance from neighboring units, roadblocks, see E.6.;

   4. the seriousness of the offence;

   5. the apparent condition of the vehicle being pursued;

   6. weather and road conditions;

   7. the volume of pedestrian or vehicle traffic that is or might reasonably be expected in the area;

   8. location of the pursuit, i.e. urban or rural area;

Appendix I (continued)

9. length of time/distance involved in the pursuit; and

10. are there any limits on the member's ability to operate the police vehicle.

5. In the interest of your own safety:

1. Call for additional police units and provide a description of the suspect vehicle.

E. 5. b   5. 2. Notify your telecommunications center of your location and intended action, and initiate a CPIC query before stopping a vehicle.

3. Arrange to recontact your telecommunications center at a time agreed upon

EXCEPTION: Record vehicle data when you are unable to contact

Appendix I *(continued)*

E. INVESTIGATIVE TECHNIQUES (cont'd)

E. 5. a. 7 (cont'd)

behind the first pursuing police vehicle to provide any necessary backup assistance.

8. No criticism will be leveled against a member whose judgment dictates the need to discontinue a hazardous pursuit. However, criticism will follow when a pursuit is initiated and continued unnecessarily, particularly if death or injury results.

9. A pursuit will be abandoned when the risk to anyone becomes too great, when the pursuit becomes futile or apprehension by other means is possible.

10. A decision to abandon a pursuit may be made by:

1. the driver of a police pursuit vehicle,

2. the senior member directly involved in the pursuit, or

3. a supervisor monitoring the progress of the pursuit.

Appendix I *(continued)*

E. INVESTIGATIVE TECHNIQUES (cont'd)

E. 5. d. 3. 1. A copy of the RCMP-wide recapitulation report will be made available to COs and the Solicitor General of Canada.

E. 6. **Roadblocks**

E. 6. a. **General**

    1. A roadblock is set up only:

        1. to prevent the escape of a person who may be lawfully arrested for a serious criminal offence,

        2. to prevent a reasonable foreseeable threat of death or grievous harm to a member or other person, or

        3. if the roadblock will not endanger the lives or safety of other persons.

    2. A roadblock is not to be used when there is an innocent person in the fleeing vehicle.

    EXCEPTION: In some hostage situations, a roadblock may be the only method of stopping a vehicle.

    3. For the purposes of this subsec.:

        1. A **barrier** is the partial blocking of a roadway to ensure the slowing of all vehicles, e.g. two police cars placed diagonally on the roadway a short distance apart forcing vehicles to maneuver between them.

        2. A **barricade** is the total blockage of a roadway to prevent the passage of vehicles.

E. 6. b. **Member**

    1. Before setting up a roadblock (including any barrier or barricade), consider the following:

        1 other means that may be available to apprehend the subject, e.g. arrest at a later time through other procedures;

Appendix I *(continued)*

E. 5. b. 5. 3. EXCEPTION (cont'd)

    your telecommunications center.

6. Do not use a vehicle to ram or force a suspect vehicle off the roadway unless the:

    1. use of such force is fully justified and no lesser means are possible,

        NOTE: See III.2.J. regarding the discharge of a firearm at a vehicle.

    2. occupants of the vehicle are committing an indictable offence, and

    3. the public will be seriously endangered if the vehicle is not stopped

7. After each hazardous pursuit, complete form 2088 for review by your commander.

E. 5. c. **Commander**

1. Ensure the hazardous pursuit directive is brought to the attention of all members.

    1. Implement a form of sign-off ensuring that a member acknowledges he/she has read and understands the directive.

    2. Conduct debriefing sessions after all hazardous pursuits to review procedures and to verify whether there was compliance with the directive.

    3. Review form 2088 and write on the form your comments on the merits of the pursuit and forward it to div. headquarters.

E. 5. d. **Division**

1. Analyze form 2088 for compliance with existing directives, and if necessary initiate follow-up action.

2. When a pursuit causes death or serious injury, immediately forward particulars by message or fax to the A&PO, with a copy to Headquarters, ATTN: National Operations Centre.

3. Before the end of January, recapitulate on form 2438 all the hazardous pursuits for the previous calendar year and forward it to Headquarters, ATTN: OIC Contract Policing Br.

Appendix J

RCMP GRC	POLICE MOTOR VEHICLE ACCIDENT REPORT **CONTINUATION**	RAPPORT D'ACCIDENT – VÉHICULE DE POLICE **SUITE**	15-2134	DIV, FILE NO.– Nº DE DOSSIER DIV.

- ORIGINAL TO DIVISION L'ORIGINAL À LA DIV.
- COPY TO DETACHEMENT UNE COPIE AU DÉTACHEMENT

PFB / CMP / P-PU-075
F.R.P GRC

P.M.V. CODE – CODE DU V.P.

DIV.	SP-CAR. Marg	Make Marq	YR ANN.	SEQUENCE Nº D'ORDRE
E	KIKC	3	18	15

DATE OF ACCIDENT
DATE DE L'ACCIDENT

YEAR ANNÉE	MONTH MOIS	DAY JOUR
93	12	24

TIME – HEURE (i.e. 17 h 03/04 h 47) (P. ex 17 h 03/04 h 47)
21 h 18

OTHER VEHICLE OPERATOR – CONDUCTEUR DE L'AUTRE VÉHICULE

NAME OF OPERATOR – NOM DU CONDUCTEUR
MICHELL, RUSSELL THOMAS
D.O.B. – D.D.N. 1962-MAY-30

ADDRESS - ADRESSE
BRIDGE RIVER RESERVE LILLOOET, BC

VALID OPERATOR'S LICENCE NO. Nº DU PERMIS DE CONDUIRE DU CONDUCTEUR
3902372 (PROHIBITED DRIVER) PROVINCE BC

OTHER VEHICLE – AUTRE VÉHICULE

REG. NO. – Nº D'IMMATR.	PROVINCE	YR. – ANNÉE	MAKE – MARQUE	MODEL – MODÈLE	YR. – ANNÉE
3N69R9X113764	BC (EXPIRED)	OLDS	88		1979

NAME AND ADDRESS OF REGISTERED OWNER SAME AS ABOVE
NOM ET ADRESSE DU PROPRIÉTAIRE ENREGISTRÉ. MÊME QUE CI-DESSUS ☐ YES OUI ☐ OR – OU OUI ROGER LAZORE

CONDITION OF VEHICLE PRIOR ACCIDENT - ÉTAT DU VÉHICULE AVANT L'ACCIDENT
AVERAGE

INSURED - ASSURÉ ☐ YES OUI ☒ NO NON   COMPANY - COMPAGNIE ICBC   POLICY NO. - Nº DE POLICE ACE 634

EXP. DATE – DATE D'EXP 93-12-17   COVERAGE - PROTECTION $
AGENT'S NAME AND ADDRESS - NOM ET ADRESSE DE L'AGENT
McGRAW, EMPRESS INSURANCE

DAMAGES – DOMMAGES
P.M.V. - V.P.
GRILL, FRONT BUMP, HOOD
OTHER VEHICLE - AUTRE VÉHICULE

PASSENGERS IN ALL VEHICLES – PASSAGERS DES VÉHICULES (✓)

	NAME – NOM	ADDRESS – ADRESSE	PMV V.P.	OTHER AUTRE
1	CST. KEITH McKAY	c/o SNTPOLICE	☑	☐
2			☐	☐
3			☐	☐
4			☐	☐
5			☐	☐

BRIEF STATEMENT OF P.M.V. OPERATOR – BRÈVE DÉCLARATION DU CONDUCTEUR DU V.P.

Writer knew that MICHELL was a prohibited driver. Once McKAY arrived we departed the detachment for Moha Rd. where MICHELL was supposedly driving. PC 22A3 which I was driving, came upon MICHELL's vehicle approx. 12 kms N/W of Lillooet on Moha Rd. I turned my P.C. to catch up with MICHELL's vehicle. MICHELL's identity was unknown at this time. The first 20-25 kms of road were gravel with some slippery sections. MICHELL was identified at approx. 20 km mark of Slok Creek Rd. The pursuit continued with speeds between 15 kms and 65 kms/hr. Writer had expressed concern to Sgt. OLSEN of low fuel. It was decided that MICHELL's vehicle should be nudged off the road. MICHELL's vehicle was to be forced off the

OPERATOR - CONDUCTEUR
(S. R. WALSTROM) CST.   DATE 94-JAN-10

A-110-1(92-09) (*)   (continued over)......   © ROUGH SKETCH ON REVERSE - CROQUIS AU VERSO

Appendix J *(continued)*

road in an area which wouldn't cause injury to anyone. Writer approached a series of corners that were flat and attempted to strike MICHELL's bumper without success. Writer closed the gap between MICHELL's vehicle and an opportunity came. The first was at about 40 km/hr. this sent MICHELL's vehicle into the ditch, right. MICHELL regained control and came back onto the roadway and writer hit MICHELL's bumper a second time sending MICHELL to the opposite ditch. MICHELL once again regained control and came back onto the roadway. The third strike was done at approx. 38 km/hr on MICHELL's right rear bumper. MICHELL's vehicle went left, into the ditch and came back onto the roadway. Meanwhile writers P.C. completed 180 degree turn and left the roadway, left and went into the ditch backwards. The vehicle was stuck at that point. The area where this occurred was slightly downhill and compact icy snow and writer attempted to brake but was unable to.

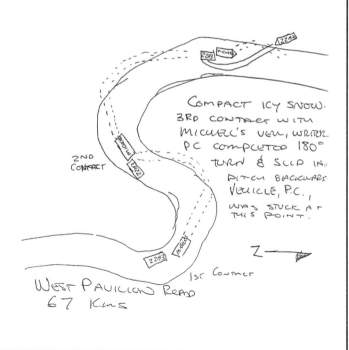

Index